Complete Relaxation

Complete Relaxation

By Steve Kravette

Illustrated by Plunkett Dodge

1469 Morstein Road
West Chester, Pennsylvania 19380 USA

Complete Relaxation
by Steve Kravette

Copyright © 1979 by Steve Kravette
Illustration Copyright © 1979 by Para Research, Inc.

International Standard Book Number: 0-914918-14-1

Designed by Malcolm Mansfield
Typeset in 14 point Bem on a Compugraphic Editwriter 7500
Printed by W.P. on 55-pound Natural shade offset paper.

Published by Whitford Press
Distributed by Schiffer Publishing, Ltd.

This book may be purchased from the publisher.
Please include $2.00 postage.
Try your bookstore first.
Please send for free catalog to:
Whitford Press
c/o Schiffer Publishing, Ltd.
1469 Morstein Road
West Chester, Pennsylvania 19380

Manufactured in the United States of America

Fourth Printing, July 1987, 3,000 copies
Total copies in print, 16,000

Dedication

To Dorothy,
whose lifework and encouragement
made this book possible.

To Carolyn,
whose love and enthusiasm
made it probable.

And to Jennifer,
whose being
made it materialize.

Contents

The beginning

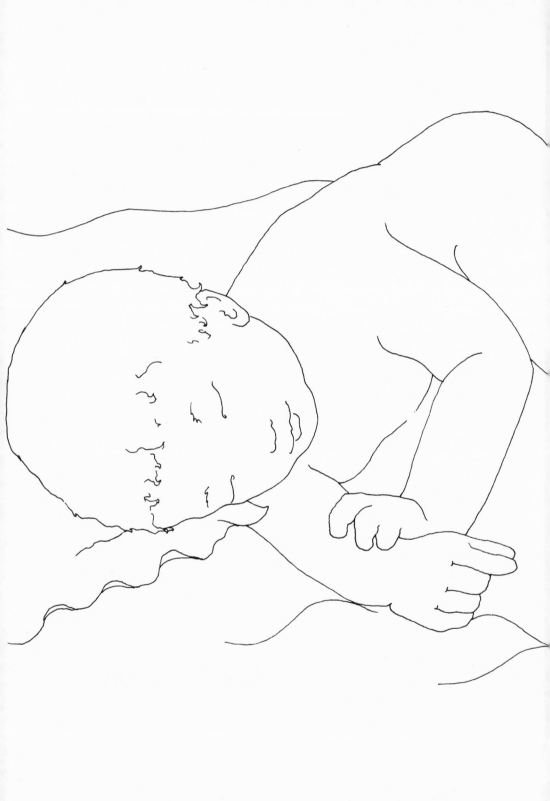

The beginning

You were born
with the capacity to use your energies
in a free and flowing way,
so you could develop your full potential
for enjoying your life
and making the most of it.

Through the years,
little by little
you lost or blocked this primal capacity.
Why you did doesn't matter now.
But as you did,
the part of you that could flow and be free
and sing and laugh and enjoy its creaturehood
stiffened,
gave up its harmony with the universe,
and became tense.

The tension came
in obvious ways you may be well aware of
and subtle ways you may still need to discover.
This book will help you explore your tension
and release it.
Through complete relaxation.

It is a book that is written
for all of you:
your breath, your body, your emotions,
your thoughts, your spirit,
and your interplay with people around you.

It's a book for all of you,
all linked together
in a way that will reopen your innate capacity
to live your life
as you were meant to live it.
More joyfully, more exuberantly,
and more completely relaxed than ever before.

It is not a book like other books,
and not a book on yoga and exercise.
In fact, you don't have to lift a finger
for this book to do its work.

It is not a book that's only for your brain
or your emotions, either.
It is for everything you are,
all together,
written in a style that your inner self
will understand and respond to,
almost automatically.

This book is complete.
And it will help you to relax completely,
which you will find to be the first step
toward opening up, growing, developing yourself,
and expanding your power and your life.

The format of this book
is a soothing series of explorations
that activate natural internalized solutions
for releasing tension.

Remember what it feels like
to be so totally pleased with yourself
that the glow of your vitality
illuminates the space all around you.
With this book
you can begin to feel much more like that
much more of the time.
Completely naturally.

Many people think they are relaxing
when they have a couple of drinks
or use drugs.
They're mistaken.
External agents can never relax you
as well as internal connections and changes.

Drinking, drugs, and all forms of escapism
dull your awareness
and lull you into believing you feel better
because your awareness has dropped
below a level
where you can perceive your tension.
The long-range effect is
to build and create more tension.
After all,
you can't possibly relax
with a splitting headache, a hung over stomach,
or a craving for pills, powders, or whatever.

The format of this book
also throws a lot of material at you
in a relatively little space.
So keep in mind
that trying too hard and not trying hard enough
both produce tension.

Find your own level and your own tolerance
for working with yourself.
Or for joining with a friend,
reading aloud softly to each other,
and working with yourselves
together.

Enjoy your explorations
and learn to sense when you've done enough
for one session.
Overdoing anything,
even relaxation,
is not relaxing.

Other than that,
just expect the unexpected.
You will feel different.
And you will feel better.
You'll feel the changes ever so slowly
at first.
But one day they will add up for you
in dramatic and astonishing ways.

You'll find you have become
more sensitive and more receptive,
more calm, more sensuous, more connected,
more in control.

Your walk and body posture will evolve.
Your voice will soften and deepen.
Your skin and muscle tone will feel better
to your own touch and to your lover's touch.
Your mind will become stronger, more searching,
more positive.

Your emotions will flow more smoothly
and they'll stabilize
so that your highs and lows will be less extreme.
You will feel more satisfied with yourself
and like yourself more than you ever have
before.

You will be
what you may never have been before.
Yourself.
Beginning now.

Becoming aware

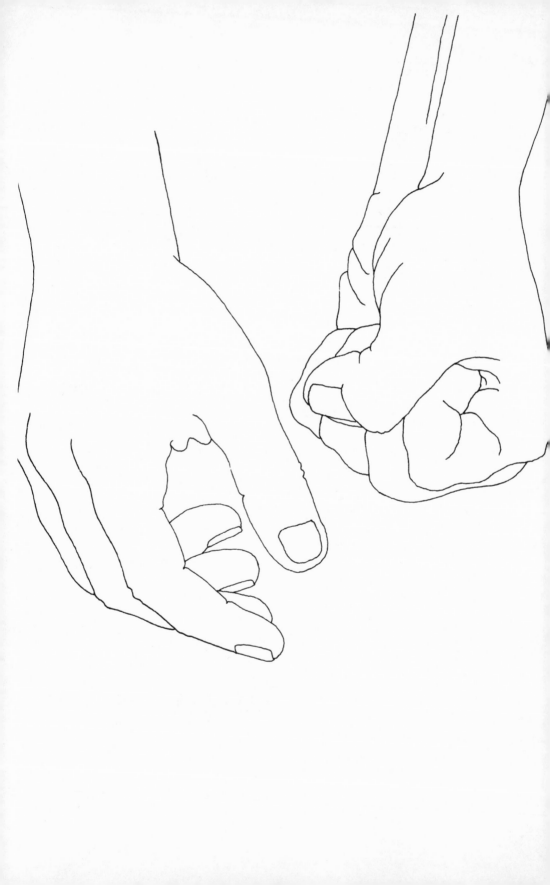

Becoming aware

The difference between relaxation and tension
is the difference between
being and doing.

You are being
when you are centered in the present,
when you are fully experiencing
the power and the energy
of the moment you are living in.
And when you are fully focused
on your own feelings and sensations,
wants and desires.

When you are being,
what you are being
is you.
When you are being you,
you can relax.

You are doing
when you are adrift in activities and energies
outside of yourself,
when your focus is snagged
on your past performance or future goals
and you are out of touch with
your own inner space.

When you are doing,
what you are doing
is mechanically trying to meet
someone else's expectations.
And because part of you knows
you can't ever do that,
you can't relax.

Whenever what you are doing
involves and merges with being,
you will do better.
And whenever what you are being
embraces and loves what you are doing,
you will be more,
because you will become
more and more expansive.

If the question is
to be
or not to be,
the answer is
to be.
But first you must
be aware.
Aware of what you are being,
feeling, thinking, and experiencing.

You must learn to be aware
of where you are flowing smoothly
in your space
and where you are tense, rigid, and constricted.
Where you feel loose.
And where you feel tight.
Where you feel terrific.
And where you feel pain or hurt
or numb.

You can begin to become aware
by letting your left hand hang loosely
and making a fist with your right hand.
And sensing the different ways
your hands feel to you.

Then reverse your hands,
making a fist with your left hand
while your right hand hangs loosely.
And feel the difference now.

That feeling and sensing process
is awareness.
And
you can't begin to relax
until you first become aware
that you are tense
and where you are tense.

Many people don't know how to tell
when or where they are tense.
But everyone can learn to do both.
By reading this book even this far,
you are well on your way.

All tension is not bad.
In fact, you need a certain amount of tension
to be fully alive.

Without tension in your body
to hold you up,
you couldn't stand or sit.
Without tension in your mind
to hold your attention,
you couldn't think.
Without tension,
you would be a blob.

So when we talk of
letting go of your tension,
we are talking about
the unnecessarily high level of tension
that practically everyone has learned to live with.

Excessive tension drains your energy
and affects you on all levels by producing
physical tightness, emotional anxiety,
mental confusion, and a spiritual void.

Excessive tension builds to a threshold
where too much is too much
and one thousandth of an ounce more
causes emotional explosions on a devastating level.
To lower your threshold of tension,
you have to first become aware
of where it's coming from. And why it's there.
What causes excessive tension?
Ask yourself.
What causes it in you?

Perhaps the tension you don't need anymore
comes from:
A runaway drive to complete things.
A compulsiveness to achieve perfection.
An inner reaction to meet all competition head on.
Unfulfilled expectations about someone else.
Someone else's expectations of you.
A feeling of alienation from yourself or others.
Excessive worries and fears.
Financial pressures and problems.
Any one of a hundred other things.

Through the heightened sense of self-awareness
this book can help you attain,
you can discover your own sources of tension
and do something about them.

Like relaxing yourself
and letting yourself be.
So you can send away tension
like a healthy body sends away infections.

Begin by checking yourself out.
Use the check-out chart on the next two pages
now.
And use it again
two more times in the next two days.
Just read each element of tension.
And check yourself to see if it fits you
right now.
Then check the chart.

If you're at home now,
write "home" at the top of the first column
and note the time of day.
Plan to be somewhere else
when you work with
the next two columns.
Perhaps
you could be
at the office, traveling, commuting,
or even in a restaurant.

The chart will tell you
some things you don't know now:

Where your excess tension is.
What form it takes.
Where it happens.
And what your patterns of tension are.
There are a few extra blank lines
where you can add your own
elements of tension
if you don't see them here.

While some tension problems may require
professional help,
chances are, with the help of this book
most of your tension
can be handled
by you.
As you let yourself be.
And as you begin
to balance moments of pressure
with moments of complete relaxation.

CHECK-OUT CHART

YOUR LOCATION

PLACE/TIME

PLACE/TIME

PLACE/TIME

TENSION LOCATION

Body tension

Breathing rapidly, irregularly, and shallowly

Tightness at back of neck

Pain at back of neck

Nervous jitters

Tapping fingers

Hand making a fist

Biting nails

Picking at yourself

Scratching

Nervous tic

Legs crossed, feet tapping

Legs crossed, feet stiff

Digestion trouble

Nibbling and overeating

Poor coordination

Backache

Shoulder pain

Elimination problems

Headache

High blood pressure

Poor posture

Skin eruptions

Tired all the time

Sexual problems or dissatisfactions

18

YOUR LOCATION

PLACE/TIME PLACE/TIME PLACE/TIME

TENSION LOCATION

Emotion tension

Depression

Angry more than one hour a day

Acting out your emotions

Feeling alienated or alone

Feeling you're not there sometimes

Thought tension

Incoherence

Forgetful

Loss of comprehension

Tendency to make mountains out of molehills

Primary focus on future goals

Primary focus on past performance

Living in the past

Other tension

_____

_____

_____

_____

_____

_____

_____

_____

_____

_____

19

Breath relaxation

Breath relaxation

Now you are starting to sense your self.
Now you are learning if you are tense.
And when you are tense.
Now you are becoming more and more aware.
And now you can begin to relax.

The balance of this book
is a series of discoveries you can make.
And explorations you can take.
Alone.
Or with a friend.

The work isn't really work.
It is not competitive.
It can be done without strain.
If you try an exploration
and you find yourself getting tired,
work to a point
just a little beyond your tiredness.
Then stop.
Rest.
And allow your body, your mind, and your emotions
to absorb
the effects of what you have done.

We learn how to be.
By relaxing
a little bit at a time.
By letting go of our tightness
and our tension
and our control
a little bit at a time.

We learn how to be.
By maintaining our awareness
and realizing:
That all of our actions are choices.
That all of our choices are ours to make.
That given the choice
of being tense or of being relaxed,
the choice is obvious.

We learn how to be.
From this point on.

Breathing

From the very first, there was breath.
You didn't have to think about it.
You just did it.
Life and breath came to you
at the same moment.
And that's all there was to it.

You were born. You took air in.
First:
Your diaphragm expanded.
Your ribs separated.
Your chest rose.
Your lungs filled.
From the bottom-most part to the top.

And then:
Your diaphragm flattened.
Your ribs came together.
Your chest lowered.
You gurgled. Or cried. Or yelled. Or cooed.
You were alive.
You were breathing.
You were being.

If you don't breathe that way anymore,
you don't feel that way any more.
You can't feel
as relaxed as babies and puppies
and small animals feel,
unless you breathe
the way babies and puppies
and small animals breathe.
Try it now.

Your lungs

Visualize in your mind
both of your lungs as a pear-shaped balloon.
The widest part is on the bottom.
And it includes your diaphragm.
Inhale through your nose.
Fill the balloon
from the widest part on the bottom
to the narrow neck of the pear
on the top.

Tie an imaginary string
around the stem of the pear.
And hold the balloon full for a moment.

Then untie the string.
Let the air out all by itself
as you allow yourself to exhale
through your nose.
In your mind,
follow the path of the air as it leaves.

And sense the balloon contract.
And sense the balloon relax.

Your basic relaxation breath

Place your hands just under your ribs
with your fingertips touching.
Bend over from the waist.

Inhale through your nose.
And send all the air to your fingertips.
Feel them separate as your diaphragm expands.
Then feel your ribs separate.
And sense your chest expanding.
Hold your breath for a moment.

Then release your breath.
As you exhale through your nose,
feel your fingertips come together
as your diaphragm flattens.
Sense your ribs coming together.
And feel your chest lower.

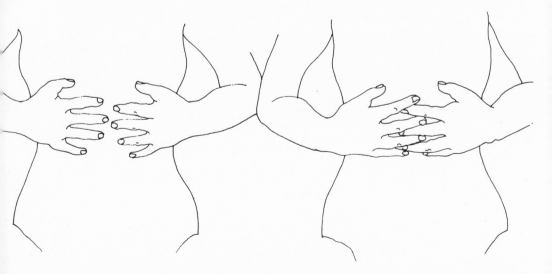

Repeat this same breathing sequence
until it becomes natural, comfortable, and easy.
And then try it again standing straight and tall.
This is your basic relaxation breath.
The breath that is the beginning
of being.

By using your basic relaxation breath
and variations built upon it,
you can be.
You can be fully and completely what you are.
You can clear yourself of worry, fear, and doubt.
You can control many of the automatic functions of your body.
You can restore the energy balance within your body.
You can warm yourself when you feel cold.
And cool yourself when you feel warm.
You can revitalize yourself when you feel drained.
You can loosen any part of you that feels tight.
Very easily.
And very simply.
As you'll see.
All throughout this book.

Clearing yourself

Lie down on your back.
Uncross your legs.
And let your hands rest at your sides, palms up.

Think about something that is bothering you.
Let it develop into a worry or a fear.
Then place your hands just below your ribs
and just above your waist.
Breathe your basic relaxation breath.

First inhale to a silent count of five.
Hold for a silent count of five before you exhale.
Exhale for a count of five.
Hold for a count of five before you inhale again.
Think only of your breath.
And the rhythmic counting cycle of your breathing.

Send all other thoughts away.
And sense the relaxation flowing through you.
And sense the worry and doubt and tension leaving you.
As you repeat your inhale,
        and repeat your hold,
        and repeat your exhale,
        and repeat your hold,
        to the count of 6,6,6,6.
Repeat it all again to the count of 7,7,7,7.
And again,
to the count of 8,8,8,8.

Now explore yourself.
And become aware of how you feel.

And consider this:
The more slowly you breathe, the more relaxed you become.
The more rapidly you breathe, the more tense you become.

When you breathe through your nose,
you breathe more slowly
because the filters in your nose slow down
each inhalation and each exhalation,
allowing your basic relaxation breath to clear your mind.

Controlling your body processes

Right now.
Stop whatever you're doing.
And take your pulse.
You'll find it on the inside of your wrist,
or along the side of your throat
about three inches below your chin.

Hold your pulse with your fingertips for fifteen seconds.
Count the beats.
Multiply by four.
Remember the total.
Lie down on your back.
And breathe your basic relaxation breath for three minutes.

Let all outside thoughts pass through your mind.
And out of your mind.
Send them on their way with each exhale.
Think only of your breathing.
And how marvelous it feels to let each breath you take
refresh and restore your body.
Then take your pulse again.
You'll find it at least twenty percent slower.
Maybe more.

You can slow your whole body down
with your basic relaxation breath.
Your pulse, your heart, your circulation,
your blood pressure.
And like any system,
you'll run longer if you run slower.

Through breathing, you can be
as fully integrated as you were as a baby.
You can sleep like a baby.
And digest your food like a baby.
And laugh spontaneously like a baby.

And you can be
that way
for a long, long, long, long time.

Restoring your energy balance

Very seldom,
if at all,
is your energy evenly distributed throughout your body.
It tends to run or jump
here or there.
And get stuck occasionally.
Tension is energy that is stuck.
Energy that can't flow freely through you.
Your breathing can release the binds.
Like this.

Sit in a comfortable position.
Sense your spine as straight as it can be.
Breathe two or three basic relaxation breaths.
And then:

Inhale.

Place the first two fingers of your right hand
just between your eyebrows.
Close your right nostril with your thumb.
And inhale through your left nostril for four counts.

Close your left nostril with the last two fingers
of your right hand
and hold both nostrils closed for sixteen counts.

Hold.

Open your right nostril
by releasing your thumb
and exhale to the count of eight.

Exhale.
Inhale.

Inhale immediately through your right nostril
to the count of four.
Close both nostrils and hold your breath
for sixteen counts.
Open your left nostril
and exhale for eight counts.

Repeat the entire cycle
two more complete times.

Hold.

Close your eyes.
And sense the perfect balance of energy
in the left and right sides of your body.

Become aware of how good you feel.
You may want to vary the sequence
to the count of 2:8:4 or 6:24:12.
And discover
where your own best balance point can be found.

Warming yourself

When you feel cold,
begin your basic relaxation breath.

Exhale.

Slowly increase the tempo of your breathing.
Inhaling and exhaling just as deeply as before.
But faster and faster and faster and faster.
In and out.
And in and out and in and out.
And in and out and in and out and in and out and
in and out.
Until you feel your body warming.

As you breathe this way,
your breath becomes a bellows.
Fanning the fire deep within you.

Cooling yourself

When you feel warm,
your breathing can cool and refresh you.
Because the air outside of you
is cooler than your body temperature,
you can create a refrigeration effect.
Like this.

Place your tongue against the roof of your mouth.
And take short panting inhalations through your mouth.
Close your mouth.
Hold your breath in.
Let the coolness flow through you.

When you can't hold any longer,
exhale through your nose.

Repeating this cycle two or three times
will cool you down.
And relieve your thirst.

Revitalizing yourself

Revitalizing your body without stress
is a matter of life and breath.

Stand up.
Inhale your basic relaxation breath
as you make fists with both hands
and bring them to your chest.
Hold your basic relaxation breath
as you stretch your arms out to each side,
opening up your entire chest.

Still holding your breath,
clasp your hands behind your back.

As you exhale,
bend over
bringing your forehead toward your knees
and your hands way over your head.

Then,
as you inhale again,
use your arms as a lever
to help you slowly unwind your spine.
And stand,
keeping your chin tucked in to your chest.

When your spine is straight
let your head become erect,
and exhale slowly.
Become aware
of the incredible supply
of fresh energy
flowing through you.

An instant relaxation

Wherever you are,
whenever you feel tense all over,
blink your eyes shut.
And visualize yourself
on a beautiful island.

Build the image as you inhale
your basic relaxation breath.
And as you exhale,
see yourself completely relaxed
with all the tension leaving your body.

One breath of fresh air from your island
is all it takes.
But you may stay for as long as you like.

Another instant relaxation

When you feel tight all over,
make yourself feel tighter all over.

Tighten your whole body.
From your toes, through your legs,
your hips and buttocks and genitals and waist,
your stomach, your chest, and your back,
your shoulders, arms, and hands,
your neck, your face, your scalp.

Tighten everything.
Inhale your basic relaxation breath.
Hold everything.
Then exhale and send all the tension away.

Feel the freedom of letting the tightness go.
And feel how completely relaxed you are.

One part at a time

Find a place in your body that feels tense.
Breathe your basic relaxation breath.

As you inhale,
imagine that you are filling your tense place
with air.
As you hold,
imagine that all of the tension is
flowing into the air.

As you exhale,
imagine that your breath is leaving your body
through the pores of your skin
nearest the place where the tension was.
As you continue to exhale,
feel all of the tension leaving your body
with the air.

You can breathe
into any part of you
that feels tense.
And you can relax it
instantly
this way.

Body relaxation

Body relaxation

Well being
requires a well body.
A body that resists stress
and overcomes disease
by conserving
all the energy that tension drains away.

When your body is relaxed,
it allows your mind and your emotions
to relax.
Tranquilly, calmly, naturally.

No muscle
can be tense and be relaxed
at the same time.
So,
to physically relax,
you tense your muscles in a controlled way,
you sense your muscles contracting,
and then you release them.

Whenever you feel your body is tense,
any one of the explorations
you are about to read and try
will help you to relax and to feel
better.

Stretching

Stand up.
Place your feet a few inches apart.
Reach your hands towards the sky.

Stretch each fingertip towards the sky.
Imagine that you are gathering stars.
And reach.
First with one hand.
And then with the other.
Again one hand, then the other.

Now reach forward with each hand
as if you are picking falling stars from the air
before they touch the ground.
Slowly straighten up
and lower your arms.
Let them dangle loosely at your sides.
Breathe your basic relaxation breath.
Allow the relaxation to wash over you.

More stretching

Stand up.
Reach your hands towards the sky again.
Stretch each fingertip upward.
And sense the muscles in your calves.

Allow your calves to contract
until you find yourself
standing on your tiptoes.
Keep stretching.
Then drop back on your heels
and stretch a little more.
Now let your arms fall by themselves
to your sides.
And breathe your basic relaxation breath.

Circle stretching

Stand
with your feet slightly apart.
Clasp your fingers together.
And raise your hands over your head,
palms toward your head.

Turn your palms up.
And keep reaching.

Become aware of the muscles
all along your shoulders
and the backs of your arms
as the stretch flows through them.

Now visualize a ball bearing inside your waist.
And rotate your arms in a circle
by stretching them all the way
around to the left side.
And straight out in front of you.
And around to the right.
And up and back.
As the ball bearing at your waist
rotates in its socket,
stretch your arms all around
another full circle to the left.
And then
two more full circles to the right.
Let your arms fall loosely to your sides.
And breathe your basic relaxation breath.

Side stretching

Stand.
Stretch your left arm straight up
alongside of your ear.
Stretch your left arm
down toward the right
with your palm down.
Bend at your side towards the right
as far as you can.

Turn your left palm up.
And push back up against the force.
Slowly bring your arm down at your side.
As you pause
and breathe your basic relaxation breath,
sense the difference
between the way your left side feels
and the way your right side feels.

Now stretch your right arm straight up
alongside of your right ear.
Stretch your right arm
down toward the left
with your palm down.
Bend at your side toward the left
as far as you can.
Turn your right palm up.
And push back up against the force.
Slowly bring your arm down at your side.

Breathe your basic relaxation breath.
And become aware of
how completely balanced both of your sides are.
And how completely relaxed you feel.

Hanging out

Stand.
With your legs loose and slightly apart.
Let your head and upper body
hang forward.
Let your arms hang loosely,
your fingertips approaching the floor.
Just hang around.
Keep dangling.
Let everything hang loose and relaxed.
As you breathe your basic relaxation breath.

Going for a swing

Stand straight
with your feet a foot or two
apart.

Let your arms hang loosely at your sides.
Let your body relax.
Allow it to let the tension go.
Then
begin to swing your arms
from side to side.
Side to side.
Side to side.

Twist your body gently,
so you can look over your left shoulder
and then over your right.
Lift your arms and swing high.
Lower your arms and swing low.
Swing at your own rhythm.
Ever so gently.
With your body and neck
loosening and relaxing.
Come to a rest whenever you want.
Breathe your basic relaxation breath.
And notice how good you feel.

Neck stretching

A pain in the neck
is your body's way of asking
for help releasing tension.
Ignore it
and more and more of you will tighten up.
Or let it go.
Like this.

Rest your chin on your chest.
Slowly bring your head all the way back.
And slowly bring it all the way forward.

Slowly
roll your head to your right shoulder.
And lower your left shoulder.

Slowly
roll your head back as far as it will go
and bring your bottom lip over your top lip.
Hold.

Slowly
roll your head to your left shoulder.
And lower your right shoulder.

Slowly
roll your head forward
and rest your chin on your chest.

Make one more slow, full circle.
Rolling your head around to your left shoulder
and back, bringing your bottom lip over your top lip.
And rolling your head around to your right shoulder
and forward.

Raise your chin.
And roll your head slowly
from side to side
and side to side
as you breathe your basic relaxation breath.

Shoulder stretching

Place your fingers on your shoulders.
And raise your elbows
alongside your face.
Push your elbows back,
bringing your shoulder blades together.
Lower your elbows to your sides.
Then bring them up again,
slowly,
alongside your face.

Continue making slow circles this way.

Then reverse the circles
and make them the other way.
Bringing your elbows down to your sides,
and way back
pushing your shoulder blades together,

and forward,
and down.

Let your arms dangle at your sides.
Shake your hands as you
breathe your basic relaxation breath.
And feel the tension pour out of your fingertips.

Shaking

Stand.
Lift your left foot and shake it.
Shake it hard.
Let the shaking spread
up through your ankle, knee, and thigh.
Rest.

Lift your right foot and shake it.
Shake it hard.
Let the shaking spread
up through your ankle, knee, and thigh.
Rest.

Shake your left hand.
Let the shaking spread
all the way up your arm.
Rest.

Shake your right hand.
Let the shaking spread
all the way up your arm.
Rest.

Shake both hands and arms.
Let the shaking spread through your shoulders.
And into your whole body.

Shake every part of you that moves.
Shake gently
and feel all the tension shaking out of you.

Come to a rest. Slowly.
Slowly.
Breathe your basic relaxation breath.
And become aware
of the relaxation tingling through your body.

Slow pacing

Stand
with your knees slightly flexed
so that your spine and neck and head
feel perfectly straight.

Balance your weight on each foot
evenly
between your heel
and the inner marginal ball
that's just behind your big toe.
Lift your toes
and experience the balance.

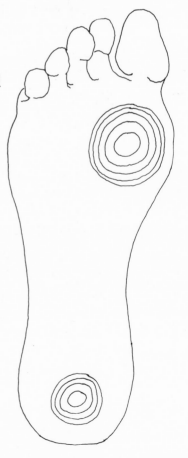

Plant your right foot firmly.
And lift your whole left foot
and bring it down
about six inches in front of your right foot,
flexing your left knee slightly.

Plant your left foot firmly.
Shift all your weight onto it.
Lift your whole right foot
and bring it down
about six inches in front of your left foot,
flexing your right knee slightly
as you shift your weight onto
your right foot.

Pace slowly just like this,
balancing your weight
over your inner marginal ball and heel.
And feel how the pacing relaxes you.

Walking

Take your body out for a walk.
Balance your weight
as you did when you were pacing.

Lift each foot as a unit,
heel and sole together.
Bring each foot down as a unit,
heel and sole together,
flexing your knee slightly.

Let your arms swing loosely
in opposition to each leg.
Left foot forward, right arm forward.
Right foot forward, left arm forward.

Time your basic relaxation breath
to as many steps as you like.
Sense the rhythm you are creating in the world.

Walking this way
benefits and relaxes
every part of you
because the motion of your arms
gently massages each muscle
all along your spine.

Sense yourself
beginning to feel marvelous.

Jogging in place

Sometimes,
physical tension comes
from an almost instinctive mechanism
that tells your body to run
when you feel afraid.
So when you feel anxiety
and your body tells you to run
and you resist the impulse,
tension builds.
And freezes inside of you.

To release the tension,
simply give in
to the old impulse.
And run.
Just stand up.
And raise each foot,
bringing your knee towards your chest.
Raise the opposite arm
with your elbow loosely bent
each time.

Run in place
for as long as you like.
When you want to stop,
stop.

Straighten up.
And grasp for stars with both hands.
Then bring your arms down
and breathe your basic relaxation breath
slowly,
three or four times,
to slow you down again.

Sports

Playing
releases tension.
And relaxes you.
Whether you want to try
swimming, running, bicycling, canoeing,
tennis, baseball, whatever,
the principle is the same.

Before you take an action,
you contract your muscles
in preparation.
Become aware of the contraction.
And inhale your basic relaxation breath.
And hold.
As you complete the action,
you release your muscles.
Become aware of the feeling of release.
And exhale your basic relaxation breath.

It works
whether you're paddling, pedaling,
backstroking, serving, or batting.
Begin to time your breathing
to your action.
And see how much better you play
and how much better you feel.

Hatha yoga

Yoga means union.
The union of body and mind and spirit.
Hatha means balance.
Balancing the body to make the union strong.

For thousands of years,
yoga postures
have been putting just the right amount of pressure
on organs, glands, and muscles
to stimulate them,
and balance their interaction.

From the internal balance
of your body working
in harmony with itself,
and from the stretching
that releases tension from your muscles,
relaxation flows softly and easily.

The yoga inverted pose

Lie on your back
on a carpet or soft mat.

Bring your knees up toward your chest
and place your hands by your side,
palms down.

Put pressure on your palms and fingertips
as you straighten your legs in the air.
Allow your legs to continue up over your head.
And rest them in a forty-five degree position
with your knees over your eyes.
Support your back with your hands.

And sense the relaxation drift over you
as you breathe your basic relaxation breath.

When you are ready to come down,
bend your knees again
and unroll your back
slowly,
one vertebra at a time.
Keep your head on the floor
until your feet have touched.
Then let your body sink into the floor.
The floor will hold you up
while you breathe your basic relaxation breath
again.

The yoga bridge

Lie on your back.
Bend your knees
and bring your heels near your buttocks.

Press your buttocks into the floor.
And then lift them.
Press your lower back into the floor.
And then lift it.
Press your middle back into the floor.
And then lift it.
Press your upper back into the floor.
And then lift it.

Arch up,
balanced on your feet and shoulders.
Inhale.
And hold.

As you exhale,
unroll your spine into the floor
one vertebra at a time.

Breathe your basic relaxation breath
and feel your body sinking into the floor.

Arica

Arica is an institute
with centers throughout the country,
teaching that man was born to be
natural and spontaneous.
That man is conditioned
into fixed tension-producing behavior
by society.
And that he can recondition himself
to be again
as free as a baby,
while still drawing upon
all the knowledge he acquired
as an adult.
Beautiful.

The Arica stretch

Stand
with your feet about six inches apart.
Relax your arms
and clasp your fingers in front of you.
Inhale deeply through your nose
and imagine your arms floating up.
Let them float up on your breath.
Then, bring your clasped hands
up and over your head.
Raise your elbows as high as they'll go.
And with your palms touching and fingers pointed down,
reach towards the middle of your spine.

As you exhale slowly through your nose,
apply pressure on your palms.
Push your hands straight up. And stretch.
And let them fall loosely
in front of you.
Breathe your basic relaxation breath.
Become aware of the integration inside of you.

Bioenergetics

According to bioenergetic psychology,
your body presents an outward picture
of the individual inside.

Your body carries
and reveals
your life history
chapter by chapter.
And your body never lies.

Tension disturbs and distorts bodies.
So a series of therapeutic
breathing and stretching techniques
has been created
to release your tension blocks
and to restore your body
by freeing trapped energy,
clearing out trapped emotions,
and generating a new and stress-free
environment for living in your self.

The bioenergetic bend

Stand
with your feet at shoulder width,
toes turned slightly inward.

Connect with the ground.
Send roots down from your feet,
anchoring you where you are.

Make fists
and push your knuckles into your lower back
as you lean back.
Arch your back as far as you can,
but keep your head straight
and your neck loose
as you breathe twenty long, slow, deep breaths
through your mouth
into your belly.
Make a sound with each exhale.
Make each sound last a long time.
Feel your body vibrate.

Let your legs remain as they are,
and bend forward
with your head and arms
dangling loosely at your knees.
Breathe another twenty long, slow, deep breaths
through your mouth into your belly,
making a sound with each exhale.

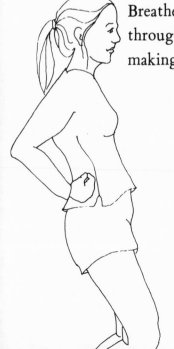
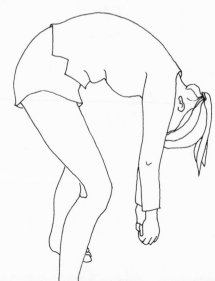

Let your legs shake all they want.
Your roots will hold you up.
Let yourself vibrate.
Let all the tension leave your body.
Let any emotion you feel
wash through your body and out of it.

Stand up again.
And breathe your basic relaxation breath.
Experience how completely different you feel.

Tai Chi

Letting go of your body.
Drifting.
Flowing openly and gently in space.
Becoming relaxed enough
to allow your life force
to permeate your entire body.
These are the goals
of an ancient Chinese pathway
to being.

Tai Chi movements are slow
and filled with grace
like an underwater ballet.

Each step is practiced
as if you were a single entity
living right now and only now.
In this present moment of existence.

The Tai Chi sway

Stand
with your feet at shoulder width
parallel to each other
and your hands dangling at your sides.
Let your knees bend forward
very slightly.

Slowly shift your weight
onto your right leg
with your knee directly over your foot.
Hold.
And breathe your basic relaxation breath
three times.

Stay on the same horizontal line
and slowly
push your weight off your right leg
and onto your left leg.
Feel your right leg grow lighter.
Feel your left leg grow heavier.

Imagine water
flowing out of one leg
and into the other.
Hold.
With your weight on your left leg,
breathe your basic relaxation breath
three times.

Keep shifting your weight
slowly
back and forth, back and forth.
As many times as you like.

Dip each knee lower each time
as you hold
and breathe your basic relaxation breath
three times for each sway.

Become aware
of each muscle on your inner leg
as you shift your weight.

Become aware
of how connected to the ground
the heavy leg is each time.
Become aware
of being.

Dancing alone

Turn on some music.
Something soft and flowing.
Be.
All by yourself.
Listen to the music.
Really hear the music.
Become one with the sound.
Then
begin to move.

Let yourself move freely
as the music fills you.
Sense your body as you move.
Sense, especially, your pelvis.
And let it go.

Try new movements.
Move in ways you've never moved before that feel
at first
awkward and uncoordinated.
See how soon they flow
into graceful and relaxed new experiences,
as you maintain your oneness
with the music.
Afterwards,
lie down.
And breathe your basic relaxation breath.

Becoming an animal

No one
ever had to tell an animal
how to breathe.
Or how to be.
Or how to release tension
and relax.
Animals know.
And
way deep inside
part of you knows what animals know.

So think of an animal.
Any kind of animal.
And let your imagination tell you
how to be
the animal you're thinking of.

Sit like an animal.
Stretch like an animal.
Walk, trot, lope, or run like an animal.
Sniff the air like an animal.
Touch like an animal.
Eat like an animal
whatever food your animal eats.
Drink water like an animal.
Lie down like an animal.

Then breathe your basic relaxation breath.
And become aware of all the ways
you and your animal are alike.
Let your imagination
allow you to become a different animal
each time.
Learn something from each animal you are.
Experience each of them fully.
And you'll find yourself
more human than ever before.

Your own relaxation cycle

Once,
when you began,
you were living free.

You felt tension
and you let it go.
You yelled it out or cried it out.
Or kicked your feet and screamed it out.
And felt better again.

Now,
you don't do things like that anymore.
Instead,
one by one,
you create your tensions.
One by one,
you hold them locked inside of you.
And let them build.

This relaxation cycle
will return a power to you
that you may not have had for years:
the power to take your tensions
one by one
and release them.
As you create tension in your body,
you can let it go.
Starting now.

Lie down on your back
on a comfortable mat.
Or sit in a comfortable chair
with your feet flat on the floor.

Spread your legs slightly apart.
And let your hands fall at your sides,
palms up.

Breathe your basic relaxation breath.
Close your eyes.
And send your awareness
down to your feet.
Tense your feet
by tightly curling your toes.

Inhale. And hold.
As you exhale,
relax your toes and send the tension away.

Tense the backs of your legs
by straightening your feet
and moving your toes toward your face.

Inhale. And hold.
As you exhale,
relax your legs and let all the tension go.

Tense your thighs
by straightening your legs and locking your knees
and lifting them about two inches
off the floor.

Inhale. And hold.

As you exhale,
drop your legs.
And let all the tension drain out of them.

Breathe your basic relaxation breath.
And as you exhale,
forget your feet and legs and thighs
altogether.

Let your awareness drift
to your hips and buttocks and genitals
and internal organs.

Tighten your buttocks and lift them.
Inhale. And hold.

As you exhale,
relax your buttocks and let them drop,
drained of all tension.

Breathe your basic relaxation breath.
If you notice any tension from your waist down,
as you exhale,
send it all away.
And notice how completely relaxed
you are becoming.

Let your awareness
flow into your hands and arms.

Stretch your fingers out,
raising the center of your palms.
Hold for one complete breath.
Inhaling. And exhaling.

Then make fists and tense and clench.
Straighten your arms and fists
about two inches away from your body.

Inhale. And hold.
Tighten your forearms and upper arms.

As you exhale,
let your arms drop.
And let your hands fall,
palms up,
like gloves lying on a table, empty and still.
Completely relaxed.

Shrug your shoulders
and try to push them up to your ears.
Inhale. And hold.

As you exhale,
let your shoulders drop.
And feel how relaxed they are.

Allow your awareness to flow
into your back.
Arch your spine up
toward the sky.
Inhale. And hold.

As you exhale,
let your spine melt into your mat or chair.
And sense the relaxation
flowing through your back.

Tighten your chest and stomach.
Draw each muscle in and tense it.
Inhale. And hold.

As you exhale,
let each muscle go loose and limp.
And feel the soothing calmness flow in.

Breathe your basic relaxation breath.
And feel how completely relaxed you are
from the neck down.

Roll your head gently
from side to side.
And feel how relaxed your neck is becoming.

Breathe your basic relaxation breath.
And if you can find
any tension anywhere in your body,
when you exhale
send it all away.
And forget that you even have a body.

Let your awareness drift into your face.
Press your tongue
against the roof of your mouth,
tighten your jaw muscles
and clench your teeth.
Inhale. And hold.

As you exhale,
open your mouth wide
and yawn for a moment,
then let your mouth be.

Feel how peaceful you are,
as your lips separate slightly
and your chin relaxes completely.

Now wrinkle your nose,
mash your lips against it,
tighten your forehead,
and make ugly prune faces.
Inhale. And hold.

As you exhale,
enjoy the tingling feeling of dissolving tension
all through your face.

Now you are feeling loose
and completely relaxed.

Lie still.
And let your breathing become
deeper and deeper.

With every inhale,
you breathe new life and vitality
into your body.

With every exhale,
you breathe old residual tensions
out of your body.

When you allow yourself
to become this completely relaxed,
the process becomes automatic.
You don't have to do anything
but lie where you are.

And feel free.

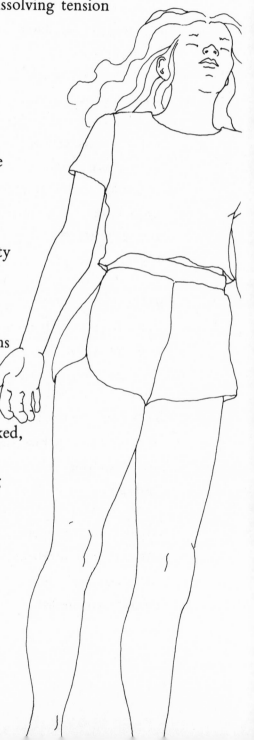

If you sense the beginning
of tension anywhere,
just deepen your basic relaxation breath.
And send it to that place.

Fill it with breath.
And let your exhalation
carry all the tension away.

You may lie where you are
for as long as you want,
feeling better than you have ever felt
before.

When you are ready to return,
count backward to yourself
from ten to one.

Your energy will return
at its own rate.
Starting in your toes and fingertips
and spreading
throughout your body.

At the count of one,
you will feel completely rested,
completely alert,
and completely relaxed.

The Relaxation Reflex

After you have experienced
the calmness and tranquility
of a complete relaxation cycle,
you can recall the feeling
completely
whenever you need to or want to
with a simple behavorial response
called
the Relaxation Reflex.

To activate the Relaxation Reflex,
take yourself through
your complete relaxation cycle once,
as you have learned it so far.
When you come to the end of the cycle,
join your thumb
and the first two fingertips
of each hand.

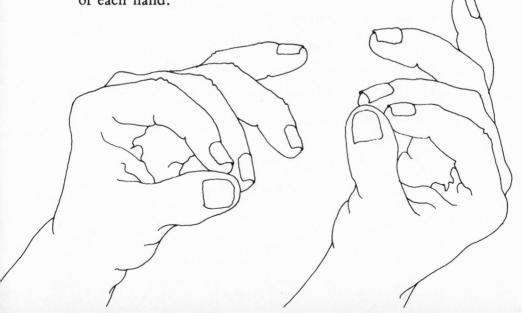

And think to yourself:
"I can return here
to this sanctuary of complete relaxation
whenever I wish,
simply by joining my thumb
and first two fingertips
of each hand
together like this,
inhaling my basic relaxation breath one time,
and on the exhalation,
saying to myself:
'Relax... Relax... Relax...' "

Now you have programmed the Relaxation Reflex
when you are fully receptive and responsive.
To activate it later,
all you have to do is
breathe your basic relaxation breath once.

As you inhale,
with your eyes open or closed,
join your thumb and first two fingers
and recall the effect of your relaxation cycle,
exploring your body from your toes to your head.
As you exhale,
say to yourself:
"Relax... Relax... Relax..."
And sense all the tension leaving you.

The Relaxation Reflex
is truly unique.

It will always center you and relax you
and bring your body, mind, and emotions
to a state of harmony and balance.

All in the span of one single breath.

Variations on the Relaxation Reflex

After you have programmed and activated
the Relaxation Reflex,
you can extend its effects
and its effectiveness
into many areas of your life,
by using variations.

For example:
If your tension takes the form of overeating
and you are developing a weight problem,
try this:

Before meals, snacks, or nibbles,
breathe your basic relaxation breath one time
with your thumb and first two fingers joined.

As you inhale,
explore your body
and recall the effects
of your complete relaxation cycle
from your toes to your head.

As you exhale,
say to yourself:
"Relax, I'm full... Relax, I'm full...
Relax, I'm full..."

Within minutes, your gnawing hunger will pass.
And your tension will vanish.
As you allow the Relaxation Reflex
to feed your need for tension-related food.

Another example:

If you smoke when you feel tense
and you would like to stop smoking,
and relax with clean fresh air
instead of burnt leaves and chemical fumes
and tar-stained fingers and teeth,
try this before you reach for a cigarette.

Breathe your basic relaxation breath once,
and join your thumb and first two fingers
together.

As you inhale,
recall the feeling
of your complete relaxation cycle
from your toes to your head.

As you exhale,
say to yourself:
"Relax, I'm clean... Relax, I'm clean...
Relax, I'm clean..."

Almost at once
a calm quiet feeling will spread throughout your body.
And your compulsive craving for a cigarette
will disappear.

Once
you have connected the Relaxation Reflex
to your complete relaxation cycle,
you can extend it to any area
of self-improvement or growth.

You can send away pain
when you are in the dentist's chair.
You can send away strain
before you make a speech to a large group.

Experiment on your own
by creating your own three- or four-word
exhalation phrase.

The Relaxation Reflex works
every time you use it
for a very simple reason:

The only way to change anything
is to stop fighting and resisting
and feeling tense all the time
about things as they are.
And to relax and flow, instead,
into things as you would like them
to be.

Sensory relaxation

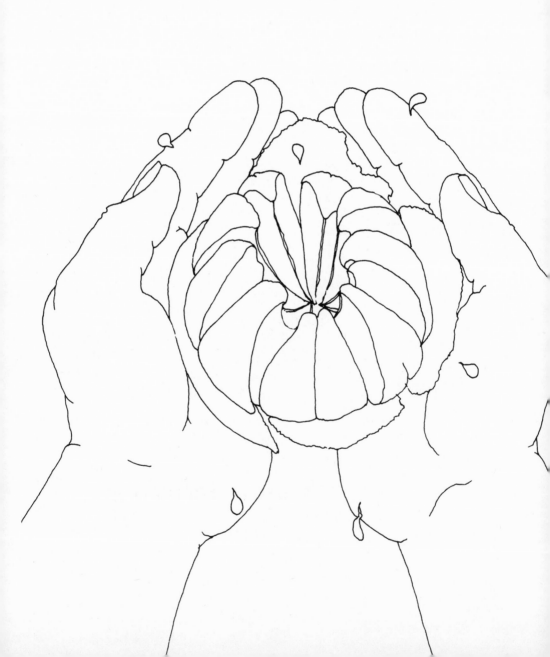

Sensory relaxation

Consider
the miraculous ways in which
you experience the world.
Sight.
Sound.
Smell.
Taste.
Touch.
Each is a channel of awareness
linking you to your environment.

When your senses are overloaded, tired,
or frazzled,
your ability to perceive
is weakened.

When your senses are relaxed,
and each can be fully focused individually,
your ability to perceive
is enhanced.
And you can exercise more control
over input from your environment
and its effect on you
and your internal systems.

Staring

Sit
in a comfortable chair,
with a mirror
at least as large as your face
facing you.

Stare,
blinking as little as possible,
at your image.
Focus on the spot
just between your eyebrows
above the bridge of your nose.

Breathe your basic relaxation breath.
And
just stare
for at least five minutes.

If you are away from home
or don't have privacy or a mirror,
sit at the window.
And stare at the sky instead.

Either way,
sense how it feels
to stare instead of to see.

Palming your eyes

Sit
in a comfortable chair
or a comfortable cross-legged position.

Place your palms lightly cupped
over each eye,
with the fingertips of each hand
overlapping on your forehead.
Seal out all traces of light
with the edges of your hands.

Stare at the soft velvet blackness
for at least five to ten minutes
as you breathe your basic relaxation breath.
Your eyes will become more relaxed,
and your vision brighter and clearer,
than they have ever been before.

Eye stretching

Sit comfortably.
And without moving your head
or straining your eyes,
look up as far as you can
and look down as far as you can
three times.

Look as far to the left
and as far to the right
as you can
three times.

Look up to the left
and diagonally down to the right
three times.

And then reverse,
looking up to the right
and diagonally down to the left
three times.

Look down
and up to the left and over the top
and down to the right,
making a large large circle.

Repeat the circle
for a total of three times to the left.
Then repeat it again
three times to the right.

Then close your eyes.
Blink a few times.
And see
how free from strain and tension
your vision has become.

Listening to music

Sit
in a comfortable chair
and close your eyes.

Listen
to a recorded piece of music
for five minutes
as you breathe your basic relaxation breath.
Immerse yourself in the music.
Listen so carefully
and so completely
that you lose all outside thoughts.

If visualizations of the music
form in your head,
send them gently away.

Just listen
and become one with the sound,
like an instrument
through which the music flows.
Tell yourself
it's all right not to hear or understand
or analyze
either the music or the experience.

Just listen.
As you let the sound
encompass you.

Afterwards,
become aware of the great and tiny wonders
of which you can partake.
By the earful.

Innersound

Sit
in a quiet place
and cover your ears with your palms.
Breathe your basic relaxation breath.
And listen to the sound inside your ears.
It's always there,
surging and rolling
like soft ocean waves lapping the shore.

Listen to your innersound
for three to five minutes.
And see how relaxed and refreshed you feel
as all irritation
from the sounds outside of you
vanishes.

If you love your innersound,
after a while
you can try sitting alone
in an absolutely quiet place,
and concentrating completely on it.
And you'll begin to hear it whenever you want
without palming your ears.
This intensifies the relaxation effect
almost magically.

Underwater sound

Lie back
in a bathtub full of hot water.
Cross your legs loosely,
so that your knees are near the faucet
and your head is supported
. by the sloping end of the tub.

Let your hands and arms float.
Let your body float and sink slowly down again
as you breathe your basic relaxation breath.
Let your ears submerge.
And listen.

The dominant sound you hear
will be the beat of your heart.

Float and drift with your eyes closed,
letting all other thoughts flow by.

Listen to your heartbeat
for three to five minutes.
And notice how completely relaxed you are.

Tongue release

Make believe
that your tongue
is a long curled-up party favor.
And roll it up
so the underside is pressed against your palate
and the tip is bent back.

Inhale
through your nose. And hold.

As you exhale,
blow out your tongue.
Let it flatten over your lower lip
with the tip as close to your chin
as it will go.
Then let your tongue curl up again
inside your mouth.

Repeat this
as many times as you like.
Become aware
that tension in your tongue
can keep you from tasting.

Tongue wagging

Stick out your tongue.
Let it enjoy the light of day.
Let it wave in the gentle air like a flag.

Let it move in every direction.
Up and down,
side to side,
in circles to the left,
in circles to the right.
Let it push against your teeth
and press up against the roof of your mouth.

Then,
as you breathe your basic relaxation breath,
become aware of the tingling in your tongue.
Notice
how relaxed it feels.

Throat relaxation

Sit
in a chair with your spine straight
and both feet on the floor.
Close your eyes
and inhale deeply.
Hold your breath
and bend your head forward,
pressing your chin into your chest.

Keep holding your breath
with your chin pressing into your chest
for as long as you can.
Then,
lift your chin. Slowly.
And exhale.

Sense what happened.
As you relaxed your throat,
you expanded your capacity to taste
and you slowed your entire body down.

See what happens
when you try this
before every meal.

Yawning

Yawn.
Make the biggest, fullest, fattest,
roundest yawn you can.
Don't apologize for it.
Sense it.
And enjoy it.
And become aware
of how easily and simply
you can relax your mouth completely.
Whenever you want to.

Nostril clearing

One blocked nostril at a time
is a normal breathing condition.
Gradually
as the blocked nostril opens,
the unblocked nostril closes
in cycles of approximately eighty minutes.
Throughout the day and night.

To open both nostrils
voluntarily
and free your sense of smell,
become aware of
which nostril is blocked right now.
If it is your right nostril,
lie on your right side
with the palm of your right hand
supporting your head
and your thumb resting on the indentation
behind your right earlobe.

Make a fist with your left hand
and push your left thumb into the floor
in front of you.

Stretch your right leg out
and bend your left leg
so that your heel is resting
on your right knee.

Remain
in this position for three minutes,
as you breathe your basic relaxation breath
and allow your right nostril to open.
If you need to,
reverse the position
and allow your left nostril to open too.

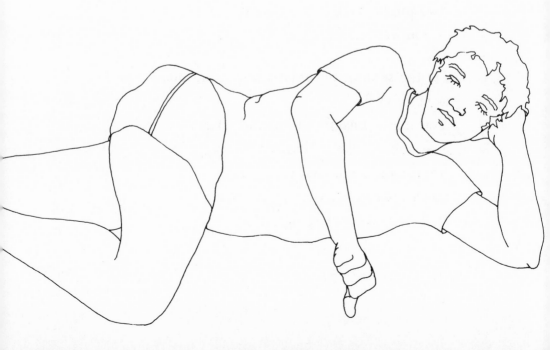

Then,
lie on your stomach,
leaning on your elbows
with your chin resting on your hands.
Become aware
of your newly awakened and heightened
sense of smell.
And the liberating feeling of release
it brings.

Tracheal relaxation

Sit comfortably
and breathe your basic relaxation breath.
Keeping your mouth closed,
allow the incoming air to make a smooth pneumatic sound
as it passes over your vocal cords.
You might imagine the sound "hum"
as you inhale.

Let the smooth pneumatic noise continue
as you exhale.
You might imagine the sound "ha".
The noise is like a hisssssssss
from your larynx and trachea,
much lower than your palate.
It sounds like a sleeping child.

Breathe this way for as long as you like.
It slows you down
as it clears all your upper breathing passages.
And isolates and releases
your sense of smell.

Shaking your fingers

Shake
your hands vigorously
until they feel light and tingling.

Touch
the three objects or surfaces
nearest you.

Sense
the heightened awareness
in your fingertips.

Energizing your touch

Sit
on your knees
and extend your arms in front of you
with your palms down.

Quickly open and close your fingers and thumbs
ten times.
Pretend you are flicking tension
off the backs of each finger.

Keep your left palm down,
turn your right palm up
and flick both hands open and closed
another ten times.

Reverse,
and with your left palm up
and your right palm down,
flick your fingers and thumbs
open and closed
ten more times.

Turn both palms up
and flick your fingers open and closed
another ten times.

Stretch your fingers back.
Then bring both palms together
until they almost touch.
Relax your fingers.
And separate your hands a little,
sensing the energy flowing between them.

Then place your hands
palms down
on your knees
and breathe your basic relaxation breath.

Become aware of the warmth
and the relaxation
flowing into each fingertip.

Touch something,
anything at all,
and sense how much more
you are in contact with it
than ever before.

Flowering fingers

Sit comfortably
and raise your forearms in front of you
palms up.
Fold your thumbs into your palms
and cover them with each finger,
one at a time,
working your way from your index finger
to your little finger.

Inhale.
And squeeze your fingers over your thumbs.

Then
exhale slowly and:
Release and stretch your little fingers.
Release and stretch your ring fingers.
Release and stretch your third fingers.
Release and stretch your index fingers.
Release and stretch your thumbs.
Stretch and hold all your fingers back
as far as they will go.
Then turn your palms down
and shake your hands gently.

Breathe your basic relaxation breath.
And notice how much more alive
and how much more relaxed
each hand has become.

Withdrawal with the Relaxation Reflex

As you contact
and isolate each of your senses,
one by one,
you can begin to relax them
by withdrawing
your awareness from them,
one by one.

You can use the Relaxation Reflex
to help you let all of your senses
be.
Without even noticing them.
One by one.

Join your thumb and first two fingers
together
as you inhale your basic relaxation breath
and recreate the feeling of
your complete relaxation cycle
from your toes to your head.

As you exhale, say to yourself
"Relax, eyes, relax... Relax, eyes, relax...
Relax, eyes, relax..."
And let yourself forget about seeing.
For the next five minutes,
you don't have to see anything.

Activate the Relaxation Reflex again
and say to yourself as you exhale
"Relax, ears, relax... Relax, ears, relax...
Relax, ears, relax..."
And let yourself forget about hearing.
For the next five minutes,
you don't have to hear anything.

Then activate the Relaxation Reflex again
and say to yourself
"Relax, nose, relax... Relax, nose, relax...
Relax, nose, relax..."
And let yourself forget about smelling.
For the next five minutes,
you don't have to smell anything.

Then activate the Relaxation Reflex once again
and say to yourself this time
"Relax, mouth, relax... Relax, mouth, relax...
Relax, mouth, relax..."
And let yourself forget about tasting.
For the next five minutes,
you don't have to taste anything.

Finally,
activate the Relaxation Reflex one last time
and as you exhale with your thumb and fingers
joined,
say to yourself
"Relax, hands, relax... Relax, hands, relax...
Relax, hands, relax..."
And let yourself forget about touching.
For the next five minutes,
you don't have to touch anything.

If you lead yourself
step by step this way
using the Relaxation Reflex
to trigger the relaxation and withdrawal
of your senses,
you'll find yourself
beginning to flow
into a form of relaxation
that takes you beyond yourself
altogether.

Thought relaxation

Thought relaxation

Your mind
is your most remarkable instrument.
It carries you
to concepts, thoughts, and actions
unachievable by any other life form
on earth.

It can lift you
to the loftiest heights
when you control it.
It can drop you
to the most miserable depths
when it controls you.

Many minds
are like instruments
which can no longer be
turned off and put away
by their owners.
They race erratically.
Like runaway powermowers,
unstoppable bulldozers,
and locomotives hurtling blindly
off their tracks.

Minds
with lost or broken on/off switches
are filled
with chatter and clutter and tension.

The explorations in this chapter
will return to you
the power to control and direct
your mind.
By repositioning
your finger on the switch
that shuts your mind off
and allows it to rest.

Each time,
you will find that when you turn your mind
back on again,
you are more alert,
more able to concentrate,
more able to use your mind productively
than ever before.

It starts here.
And now.

Thoughts

Sit
in a comfortable chair.
Close your eyes.
And breathe your basic relaxation breath.

Let yourself
step back inside yourself.
And imagine
the inside of your forehead
just above your eyes
is a large movie screen.
And you are watching your mind on it
with quiet interest.

Watch for a while
all the thoughts that race across the screen.
Don't monitor or judge the thoughts.
Or attempt to control or develop them.
Just let them be.

Let them
rush
and chatter
and bump each other across the screen
and off to one side
or the other
as new thoughts appear.

Breathe your basic relaxation breath.
And become aware
of all the undirected action
and confusion and pressure
racing across
the movie screen that is your mind.
Keep standing back.
Detatched.
Curiously watching what happens next.
Sense how your mind always tries to take over.
And how seldom it allows itself or you
to be.

One object at a time

Take any object you enjoy looking at.
Perhaps a flower,
a ring, a symbol, a sculpture,
or a design.
Set it in front of you
as you sit in a chair with your back straight.
Or in a comfortable cross-legged position.

Focus your eyes
on your object.
And keep them there,
blinking whenever you have to.

Think
only of the object you are looking at.

Notice
its color,
its shape,
its function,
the way its lines flow and blend,
its highlights and shadows.

Other thoughts will attempt
to interfere.
Send them away gently.
Just let them flow off your movie screen.

Tell your thoughts,
"I am busy now
and have no time for you.
Please come back later."
And let your mind return to your object.

Stay with it for a whole minute
at first.
Gradually,
let yourself stay with it
up to three minutes or more.

The candle flame

Sit.
On the floor
in a comfortable cross-legged position.
Or in a chair.

Place a lighted candle
two to four feet in front of you.
Fix your gaze upon the flame
as you breathe your basic relaxation breath.

Observe
how the flame flickers and dances
and moves with wondrous subtlety.

Notice the colors of the flame.
Blue on the bottom.
Dark orange at the center.
Glowing red at the wick.
Then gold
and lighter orange.

Notice
the aura of the flame,
how it spreads
and touches you with its glow.

Keep watching the flame
for about two minutes
as you breathe your basic relaxation breath.
And send all other thoughts
gently away.

Then
close your eyes.
And place your palms
lightly over your lids.
After a moment,
the afterimage of the flame
will form in the blackness as you watch.

Catch it.
And try to center it
evenly on your movie screen
on the inside of your forehead
just above your eyes.

Don't force the image.
Just let it shimmer and glow
and be.

Observe
how your flame
flickers and dances
and moves with wondrous subtlety.

If your flame disappears,
you can will it to come back to your screen.
And it will come back to your screen.

Notice the colors of your flame.
Blue on the bottom.
Dark orange at the center.
Glowing red at the wick.
Then gold
and lighter orange.

Notice the aura of your flame.

Hold the image for about two minutes.
When you let it begin to fade,
notice
the tiny changes in its form and color.

Lower your hands.
Open your eyes ever so slowly.
Sense how refreshed you feel.

Become aware
of what it's like
for your mind to be alert and relaxed,
both at the same time.

Color

Sit.
Or lie down.
Close your eyes
and breathe your basic relaxation breath.

Visualize a color.
Any color you like.
And let your breathing
become slower and deeper.

As you inhale,
visualize your color
gathering in a cloud just over your head.

As you exhale,
sense the cloud settling lower,
covering you
and spreading your color gently
over your head and body.

Keep concentrating on your color.
Letting it rise in a beautiful cloud
and settle peacefully over you.
Stay with your color
for at least ten complete basic relaxation breaths.
Discover for yourself
how each color has its own unique effect on you.

Red
is vital and lifegiving,
sometimes sensual.

Green,
especially fir tree green,
is regenerative and restorative and balancing.

Orange and gold
are energizing and warming.

Yellow
is mentally stimulating.

Blue
is cooling, spiritual, inspirational.

Indigo and violet
are idealistic and mystical.

Black
absorbs and draws inward.

White
purifies, protects, and raises consciousness.

Each color has a purpose and a time.
As you try them all,
you can discover
which colors have special meanings
and special effects on your life.
And which colors
most completely clear and relax your mind.

A silent mantra

A silent mantra
is a word or phrase
that you repeat in your mind
over and over and over.

Coordinated with your breathing,
it is a simple, yet powerful way:
To quiet your mind.
To slip below consciousness
to a level even more relaxing than sleep.
To free yourself
from practically every form of mental tension
known to man.

Dr. Herbert Benson's Relaxation Response
is one silent mantra technique
in which your mantra is simply
One... Two...

Transcendental meditation
is another silent mantra technique
in which your mantra
is matched to you
by a TM instructor.

Try it now,
and sense the magic working in your mind.

To begin,
sit
with your spine erect
in a comfortable chair.

Uncross your legs
and place both feet on the floor.
Place your hands in your lap,
with your fingers unclasped.
Loose and relaxed.

See yourself completely relaxed.
Feel yourself completely relaxed
from your head
all the way down to your toes.

Let wave after wave of relaxation
wash over you
each time you exhale.
Let the waves carry
all your tension, pressure, fear, and worry
away.
Concentrate only on your breathing
as you breathe your basic relaxation breath
slowly and deeply,
slowly and deeply.

Let your breathing deepen even more.
And begin to say to yourself
your silent mantra
in rhythm
to each inhale
and each exhale.

You could try this mantra:
Hum... So...
It means
I am the one.
Say HUM
with every inhale.
And say SO
with every exhale.

Or you could try this mantra:
One... Two...
ONE as you inhale.
TWO as you exhale.

Or you could try
any peaceful or beautiful thought.
Like:
I AM (inhale)
LOVED (exhale).

Or:
I AM (inhale)
FILLED WITH LIGHT (exhale).

Or:
RE- (inhale)
LAX (exhale).

Just sit.
Just be.
And breathe your basic relaxation breath,
repeating your silent mantra
over and over,
and over and over,
and over and over.

If any thoughts intrude,
send them gently away
or let them drift off your movie screen,
leaving it blank.
Say to yourself, "Oh well..."
And return to your mantra.

This exploration,
twice a day,
for ten to twenty minutes each time,
will help you
gain and keep control
of your mind's on/off switch.
And allow your mind
to let the rest of you
be.

Anywhere

Usually,
you don't need anything
to relax your mind
but
a different way of looking at
wherever you are.

If
you're on a subway or bus,
in a waiting room,
at a meeting,
surrounded by a noisy party,
or anywhere else
and you feel tension building,
stop what you're doing.
And do this:

Just focus your eyes
on any single point or object,
even the floor.

And breathe your basic relaxation breath
as you become aware of
that one single point.
And nothing else.

Even one or two breaths
as you focus on your point
will re-center and relax you.
And the more you try it,
the more it works.

Experiencing

All day long
and all night long,
you can relax your mind anywhere you are.
Simply by being
anywhere you are
and involving yourself
fully
in anything you are doing
at that one moment in time
that you are living.
Now.

Experience now. And only now.
And experience all the power you have
in the center of your nowness.
Everything,
every moment of your life,
is always now.
Not tomorrow or next week.
Not yesterday.
Now.

Take, for example,
something tedious or unpleasant.
Like washing dishes.

As you wash,
don't think about
what you'll do when you finish.
And don't think about
how many dishes you've already done
over the course of your lifetime.
Be
right where you are.

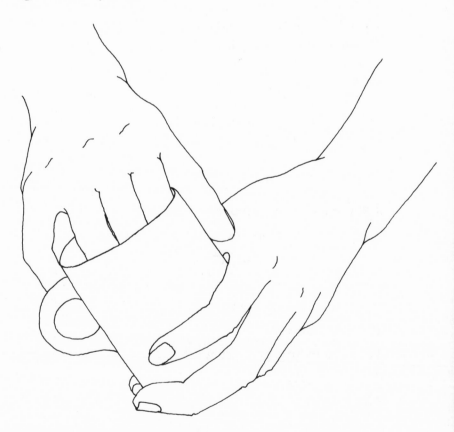

Experience the water
flowing over your hands.
Experience the difference
between the gritty texture of a dirty dish
and the squeaky smoothness
of a clean dish.
Experience the warm soap
between your fingers.

You can't be
where you're not.
You can be
where you are.
So be there.

Don't change anything.
Just become one with your actions.
Integrate yourself with them.

Experience
all of where you are
all the time.
And relaxation will follow you
wherever you go.

A sound mantra

Sounds
and the vibrations
that certain sounds produce
can relax your mind
and keep you feeling clear
and refreshed.
When tension resounds all around you,
mantras like these
can create soothing vibrations
and harmonious calm within you.

Try sound mantras softly
or loud.
But try them.

Om.
You pronounce it long and slowly
as you exhale:

AH—OH—MMMMMMMMMMM.

Start it deep inside
with a low low note of a musical scale.

Then try higher notes.
As you sit with your spine erect,
sense which parts of your body
vibrate in tune with which notes.
Om is the universal sound.
It means everything there is.

Shanti.
You pronounce it
with both syllables accented evenly:

SHAWN—TEA.

Chant it slowly
like a little song
that you could have skipped roped to
very slowly,
as a child.

Keep the SHAN
always on the same musical note
and let the TI
fall two notes below it
or rise one note above it.

There is no right or wrong way.
Your ear will tell you what to do.

Shanti
means peace.
And it brings peace and harmony
into your life.
Chanted slowly,
you can sense the peaceful vibrations
flowing like ripples on clear water
from your innermost self
beyond the surface of your body.
Surrounding you with a sea of calm
relaxation.

Go binda.
You pronounce it just the way it looks.
And say it in a fast chant
in cycles of seven times
like this,
letting your whole mouth
move with the syllables:

GO BIN-DA, GO BIN-DA, GO BIN-DA,
GO BIN-DA,
GO BIN-DA, GO BIN-DA,
GO BIN-DA. (And the DA is very loud.)

If you say the chant over and over
for ten to twenty minutes,
with your spine straight,
the backs of your hands touching
and your thumbs pointed down,
you can release all the tension
in your face as well as your mind.
And you can keep depression and negativity
far from your mind and body.

Go binda means
mental unrest and depression,
let me be.
It is the eastern equivalent of:
Blues stay away from my door.
And it will help you to remain
happy, healthy,
and whole.

Meditating with the Relaxation Reflex

Perhaps the simplest and gentlest way of all
to send thoughts away
when they are interfering with your concentration,
is to activate the Relaxation Reflex.

Inhale your basic relaxation breath
as you join your thumb and first two fingers
together,
and recreate a total feeling of relaxation
from your toes to your head.
As you exhale, say to yourself:
"Relax, thoughts, relax... Relax, thoughts, relax...
Relax, thoughts, relax..."

In the twinkling of an instant,
you will be ready for meditation,
aware
that your thoughts
have become still.

Emotion relaxation

Emotion Relaxation

Relaxing your emotions
involves looking at them
in a slightly different way
than you may have looked at them
in the past.

Emotions don't just happen.
Emotions are what they are
as the result of an instantaneous inner evaluation
of whether something is for you
or against you.

Emotions exist internally
as floating wisps of energy,
just as chairs and grapes and kittens and flowers
exist externally.
And they are just as real.

All emotions are appropriate and valid.
But no emotions have to be acted upon.
As you become more and more aware of your emotions
and their effect on you,
you become more and more aware of
whether or not
you choose to act on them.

Some emotions,
like love, joy, and happiness,
carry positive energy charges.
Some emotions,
like anger, hurt, fear, and hate,
carry negative energy charges.

All of them are perfectly all right.
And if you let them be,
they will let you be.

Emotional tension and the anxiety it produces
are the natural results
of not allowing an emotion
to live through its normal life cycle.

Left completely on its own,
an emotion will flow and ebb freely
in and over and out of you
in ever changing patterns
as new emotions drift in
with ever changing reactions to different
people and things and events around you.

The tension starts
when you hold an emotion back.
When you deny it or disown it
or lie to yourself that you don't even feel it.

When you tell it:
"I don't feel that way."
"I shouldn't feel that way."
"It's wrong to feel that way."

As long as you realize
you don't have to act on your emotions,
it is never wrong to feel what you feel.
Just as
it is never wrong to see what you see
and know what you know.

So,
emotion relaxation
involves three processes:

Becoming more aware
of what you feel
and what you may not be allowing
yourself to feel.

Becoming more accepting
of your self
and giving yourself permission
to feel whatever you feel
and be whatever you are
at any and every moment in time.

And becoming more responsible
for your choice
to lock into an emotion
or to allow yourself
to flow on to another mode of feeling
altogether,
by releasing whatever emotion
you may have been holding back.

The next group of explorations
will show you how to do it.
Some of them may not make any sense to you
at first.
So just experience them with an open mind.
And whatever sense they make
will come to you later.

The point is:
If you keep on doing
all the same things you did last week,
you'll never feel any different
than the way you felt last week.

Try
at least one new experience every week.
Starting here.
Starting now.

Holding back

Withheld emotions can be found
in the places in your body
that feel numb
or dead or dark or heavy
instead of loose, satisfied, and alive.

The longer you have held onto an emotion,
the stronger its hold
on the part of your body where you've held it.

Most of the time,
you've held back negative emotions
like fear, sadness, anger, revenge and self-pity
because a parent or a teacher told you
it wasn't nice to feel that way
and people wouldn't like you if you did.
But sometimes,
you've held back positive emotions too,
like happiness and love and childlike wonder,
because you may have been afraid
of losing them
or they seemed inappropriate at the time.

If you've held an emotion back,
the energy charge in it is holding you back
from relaxation.

Relaxation can not possibly flow into
places that have been blocked off
and locked shut
to hold in trapped emotional energies.

So for a moment,
close your eyes
and breathe your basic relaxation breath,
and become aware of
all the places in your body
that you can't make contact with
because they feel numb or dead or heavy.

And then,
consider
that you can only hold an emotion back
because you want to.
If you didn't want to hold it,
you could let it go
as easily as you can open your hand
to release a jellybean.

Maybe holding on is a habit.
But even having a habit is a choice.
Maybe
you think it is better to hold onto something,
even when it feels tense and unpleasant,
than to hold nothing at all.

If so,
you are in for a remarkable surprise.

When you learn
to release what you are holding onto,
you will discover a fundamental truth:
There is no nothing.

Nature does not tolerate a vacuum.
Something new
always flows into you.
And through you.
And on.
And something else just as new
always flows in again
to fill the space.

Letting go

Sit
in a comfortable chair.
And breathe your basic relaxation breath.
When it feels slow and deep and regular,
send your awareness
to the one place in your body
that feels the most numb or dead
or devoid of feeling.

Try to sense what you are holding there.
If your heart is heavy,
you may find hurt there.
If your belly is numb,
you may find anger.
If your throat is unreachable,
you may find sadness.
And in your hands,
you may find rage.

Immerse yourself in your heaviest place
and talk to yourself about it for a while.

You might say if you feel hurt:
"Boy, do I feel hurt.
Oh boy, I really hurt.
I can feel pain all through my heart
and down into my stomach.
My eyes are heavy with unwept tears.
I hurt.
I hurt, I hurt, I hurt, I hurt.
My world is crumbling all around me.
Everything is dark and hopeless right now.
I feel miserable."

The idea is to really get into it.
In order to really get out of it.

So talk to yourself about it.
Tell yourself, like a friend, how it is.
And then,
look for a sound or movement
that best expresses your words.

Perhaps
a growl. Over and over, louder and louder.
Or a sob or sigh.
Or wild laughter or shouting or snarling.
Or jumping up and down, shaking your fists.
Let it come.
Don't try to stop it now.

Keep breathing as deeply as you can.
You may experience
trembling, vibration, or tears,
as the energy that is the emotion
surges through you and leaves your body
with each exhalation.

Trust your body sensations.
And surrender to them.
Let yourself vibrate and shake
as the emotion shakes loose.
Inhale.
Shut your eyes and sense what's happening
inside.

Exhale.
Open your eyes wide
and let it pour out of your eyes.
Say your sound or your words
over and over.

As you vibrate,
you'll begin to feel free
and rhythmic and alive and sexual.
And then
instead of the darkness of your trapped emotion,
you will feel lightness,
joy, contentment, and peace.

Instant letting go

Identify
whatever emotion you are feeling right now.
It's not so easy at first.
But it gets easier and easier
as you do it more and more.
Then stand up
and give your emotion a voice.
As you jump up and reach for the ceiling
six times.

If you feel terrible, shout:
I FEEL (jump for the ceiling) TERRIBLE!
And repeat the shout and the jump six times.

If you feel angry, growl:
I FEEL (jump for the ceiling) ANGRY!
And repeat it six times.

If you feel wonderful, yell it out:
I FEEL (jump for the ceiling) WONDERFUL!
Again and again, six times.

And then,
do it six times again
with this variation.
Say:
I LOVE FEELING (jump up) TERRIBLE!
Or:
I LOVE FEELING (jump up) ANGRY!
Or:
I LOVE FEELING (jump up) WONDERFUL!
Or whatever it is that you do feel
at that moment.

Love it
and accept it completely.
It's part of you.
And, very often, you
are all that you've got in this world.

Wanting

Many times,
we put ourselves down
for what we want.
We tell ourselves
that what we want is childish or crazy
or wrong or inappropriate.
And as we hold back our wants,
we trap them inside.

What we want is real, too.
Very real and very important.
Hold it back and try to disown it,
and emotional tension builds and builds.
You can't relax
until you admit to yourself that you have wants,
that you have a right to have wants,
and that your wants are part of you.
So first you identify your wants,
and then you can forget about them
and relax.

Whatever you want,
it's okay.
You don't even have
to have it.
Just as long as you accept the fact
that you want it.

To live in harmony with your wants,
learn to ask yourself:
"What do I want right now?"
Ask
whenever you experience emotional unrest.

Then give yourself
at least a ninety-second silent answer.
Like:
"I want to be the center of attention.
Right now,
I want everyone's attention riveted on me.
No one should talk but me, and then
everyone should applaud..."
And on and on.

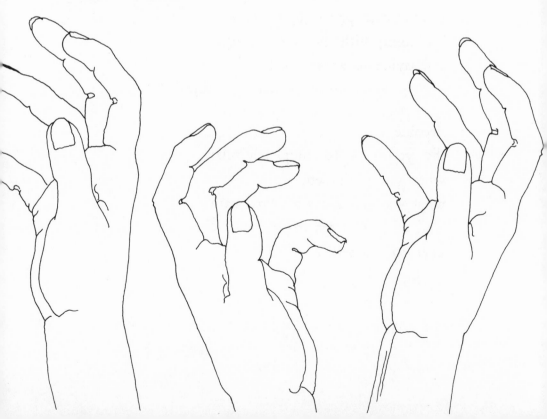

Or:
"I want the six most handsome men in this room
to fall at my feet.
And smother me with attention.
And rush to fill my glass.
And fight over
which one gets to ask me for a date
first..."
And continue on and on.

Or:
"I want everyone in this boring meeting
to vanish into thin air.
And leave me alone..."
And go on and on with it,
naming each person by name,
beginning with the most boring,
and saying to yourself
exactly where you want them to vanish to.

Become aware
that you begin to completely relax
when you can accept
what you feel and what you want.
And when you can express it.
Even to yourself.

Talking to yourself this way
as if you were a real human being,
and taking your own wants seriously
as if you were a real human being,
enables you to be a real human being.
And be
more real to everyone you meet.

Communicating wants

Maybe you find it hard
to tell people what you want
from them.
Maybe you find it hard
to say:
"I want to be cared for."
"I want to return this gift."
"I want you to take your hand off my knee."
"I want to go out tonight and not watch tv."

All the big held-back wants
and all the little held-back wants
add up to tension.
Learn to let it go,
a little at a time, like this:

Keep a small notebook.
And once a day
write down three things in it:
      1. Something you wanted.
      2. Who you asked for it.
      3. And what happened.
Just one entry a day
can lead you
to inner places of complete relaxation
and contentment.

Self approval

When you can feel comfortable
in your own space,
you will be able to maintain
emotional relaxation,
almost all the time,
almost automatically.

And you can discover
you really do have the courage
to like yourself,
regardless of what other people think.

More times than not,
the problem is not learning to like yourself.

The problem is
wanting everyone else to like you too.
And the solution is
relaxing your expectations
for approval from everyone else.

Try
making it a point to
look at the people you are with
silently
across a table,
on the street,
in an office or elevator.
And say to yourself:
"I am not going to pretend I don't like myself."

Just look everyone you see
right in the eye
and say that sentence to yourself.

Within a week,
you will discover
your need for approval vanishing.
As the approval you really needed all the time
flows from within.

Others

Right now,
say this to yourself,
or say it out loud if you are alone:
"I don't need the world to applaud
for me to be myself,
nor do I need anyone's approval.
I don't need public approval to be who I am.
I won't waste away if you don't applaud me.
I won't even waste away
if you don't understand what I am talking about.
No one MUST understand me.
What I am will prove itself
without my having to say anything."

Then,
breathe your basic relaxation breath.
And notice how free and relaxed you feel.

Needs

Three different times a day
for as long as you need,
say to yourself:

"I am not going to pretend
that my needs are not important."

Marvel
at the blissful emotional calmness
that surrounds you.

Being good to yourself

Learn to
take your pleasure
as seriously as you take your work.

Pleasure
does not have to be justified or earned.
Pleasure
is an end in itself.

Tonight,
even if you had a miserable, unproductive day,
allow yourself to give yourself a good time.
Allow yourself to go out and have fun.
And allow yourself to enjoy it.
Afterwards,
you'll feel good.
Good and relaxed.

Accepting yourself

Become aware
that you are disowning and trapping your emotions
in all the inert, energy-blocked places
in your body,
whenever you fight tension
with tension and self-disapproval.

When you fight and hate and feel ashamed
of your emotions and your emotional tensions,
you are fighting and hating
and feeling ashamed of yourself.
And you immobilize yourself.

Instead,
say to yourself:
"That tension in (my jaw or wherever),
that's me.
I give myself permission
to have a tense (jaw or whatever you have)."

Say:
"That (anger) I am feeling for her right now,
that's me.
I give myself permission to feel (angry) right now.
Even if I may choose to do nothing
or say nothing about it."

When
you let yourself be
what you are at every moment,
what you are becomes
free to change and flow and evolve.

When
you can accept yourself completely
and not always be in a hurry to change,
change will come to you
all by itself.

When
you give yourself permission
to feel negative
whenever you feel negative,
you won't feel negative for long.
And that's positively true.

Other releases

Some types of trapped emotions
are universal to human beings as a species.
And a simple sentence
said over and over like a sound mantra
can release them.

Try
any one of these sentences
that fits you.
Say it again and again
for as long as you want to
and whenever you need to.

Say over and over:
No.

Or say over and over:
I WANT.

Or say over and over:
HELP ME.

Or say over and over:
I AM TIRED OF ALWAYS BEING STRONG.

Breathe your basic relaxation breath
as you speak.
And fully experience the one thought
you are repeating.

You'll know when you've said it long enough.
You'll feel fabulous.

Listening to your body

At least three times a day,
learn to consult your body.
And become aware
of what each part of you
is saying to the rest of you.

Your hands can tell you
what emotion they may be clutching.
Your stomach can tell you
what emotion may be upsetting it.
Your throat can tell you
what emotion may be sticking in it.
Your back can tell you
what emotion may be holding you up.
Your knees can tell you
what emotion may be weakening them.

Each part of you
has its own story to reveal.
All together,
your body can tell you
everything you ever need to know
about yourself.
All you have to do is listen to it.

Negativity

You can deal most effectively
with your own negative emotional energy
by accepting it
and dealing with it directly.

You can deal most effectively
with other people's negative emotional energy
by not accepting it
and not dealing with it at all.

Try
gently stepping aside.
And letting it pass over you
like a bird or a breeze.
Or let it flow all around you like fog,
never sticking as it passes.
Detach.
Breathe your basic relaxation breath.

You'll know
when you've learned to resist
fighting back on the same level
as your attacker.
Because one of you will be completely relaxed.

From now on, whenever someone says something
intended to make you feel angry or sad,
decide whether the comment is true or not.

If it is true,
accept it constructively
and openly. And say
"That's true, that's true."
If it is not true:
Imagine the comment is a breeze
and it is blowing by.
Visualize the negativity in the form of a stone
that hurtles by as you step aside.
Say: "I feel hurt when I am misperceived this way."

Make a circle
with your thumb and your first two fingers of each hand
and activate the Relaxation Reflex.
You don't have to prove anyone is wrong.
You don't have to prove anything at all.
All you have to do is be yourself.
And be.
Time will do all the telling for you.

On-the-job relaxation

On-the-job relaxation

The working end of relaxation
doesn't involve a lot of work.

What it involves is
an easy series of explorations
and variations on previous explorations
that you can do
to shed tension and stress
during your working day,
even when you are in a roomful of people.

Each minute of the work day
that you devote to your own relaxation needs
pays off in hours
of greater efficiency,
increased productivity,
and clearer thinking on the job.

A relaxed mind and body
can flow around, with, or beyond
the people and situations surrounding you
and take you more effortlessly toward your goal.
Whether it's to go home whole at five o'clock,
or get a raise,
or make a major contribution to your field.

These explorations will better prepare you
for jangling telephones, noisy machines, and flying tensions.
These explorations will better prepare you
for the work you are doing,
whatever your work may be.

On-the-job breathing

Whenever you become aware
that your breathing has become
shallow and fast and high in your chest,
open your eyes wide
and take a good look at what you are doing.
Externally.
And internally.
Then
shift into your basic relaxation breath.
And make sure you keep it
as part of your everyday working equipment
around the office
or wherever your work happens to be.

The Relaxation Reflex at work

Relax yourself instantly
before a meeting, presentation, review for a raise,
or important phone call.

Instead of just sitting tight,
combine your basic relaxation breath
with the Relaxation Reflex.

Merely join your thumb and first two fingers
together.
As you inhale,
recreate the feeling of
a complete relaxation cycle
from your toes to your head.
As you exhale,
say to yourself:
"Relax... Relax... Relax..."
And sense the relaxation flowing through you.

Remember also,
the variations.

Before an important business lunch meeting,
you can use the Relaxation Reflex
to relax your digestion.

Join your thumb and first two fingers
as you inhale your basic relaxation breath
and visualize the full effects
of a complete relaxation cycle.

As you exhale,
say to yourself:
"Relax, stomach, relax... Relax, stomach, relax...
Relax, stomach, relax..."

To relax
your voice before you speak or present material,
use the Relaxation Reflex as you've learned it
and say to yourself:
"Relax, throat, relax... Relax, throat, relax...
Relax, throat, relax..."
Your throat will open up
and everything else will open up
to you.

As you've discovered,
the variations on the Relaxation Reflex
are endless and totally up to you.
But the effect is always the same.
And the more you use it,
the deeper it goes.

The thinker

Take a moment or two every hour,
and pretend you are
thinking about the answer
to the most enormous problem of the day.

Place your elbows on your desk,
lean your head over,
and lightly touch your first three fingertips
to the spots about two inches above
the center of each eyebrow.
These are two of the neurovascular holding points
shown in the illustrations on pages 250 and 251.
They will instantly create and release
waves of relaxation
and send them through your body.

From time to time,
also try
pressing the first two fingertips of one hand
lightly
into the spot just above the place
where your eyebrows come together.

Either way,
breathe your basic relaxation breath
with your eyes open or closed,
and gently send all the clutter in your mind
away.

Everyone will think
you are deep in thought
and about to come up with
a brilliant contribution.

The funny thing is
after just a few moments
of this exploration,
you will release so many new ideas
and become so completely relaxed,
that you probably will.

Foot work

After a few hours at work,
whether you're mostly on your feet or on your seat,
you will have accumulated tension
in your feet and ankles.

Send it away
by lifting one foot at a time
and rotating your ankle.

Make five circles to the right
and five circles to the left
ever so slowly
as you breathe your basic relaxation breath.

Be sure to give equal time
to both feet.

Lighten the workload

When you're carrying a lot on your shoulders,
you can generate a lot of stress.
Release it
at least once a day.
More if you need it.
Like this.

Sit in a chair
with both feet flat on the floor.
Lock your elbows
and press your palms down
on the seat of your chair,
allowing your shoulders to lift
towards your ears.
Drop your chin
on your chest for a moment.

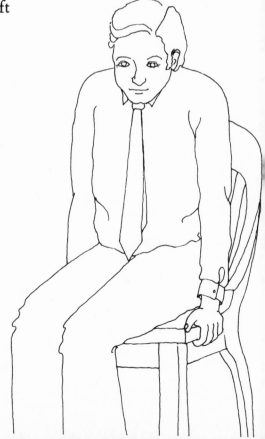

Then raise your head slowly
as if pushing against a great force.
Inhale.
And bring your head back
as far as it will go,
applying tension
and letting vibrations build up
in your neck and shoulders.

Hold your breath as long as you can.
The vibrations
will build and build and build.
And then they'll begin to subside.

As you exhale,
release your shoulders,
relax your arms,
and let your head drop forward.

Shrug off
all your on-the-job tension this way.

Stretching your breaks

Give yourself a break
whenever you want.
All you need is a few seconds.

Just
hook your fingers together
so one hand is pulling on the other.
And place both hands behind your neck,
pulling your elbows back
until your shoulder blades come together.

Sense your whole spine
stretching up.

Sense the pressure leave your shoulders
as you bring your arms down
and breathe your basic relaxation breath.

Ground-floor opportunities

Use the floor you're working on
to energize yourself and release your tensions.
First,
sit in a chair with your spine straight,
both your feet flat on the floor,
and your hands resting on your knees.
Look over your left shoulder.
Look over your right shoulder.

Let your head fall towards your left shoulder.
Let your head fall towards your right shoulder.
Let your head fall back.
Let your head fall forward.
Relax.

171

Begin to sense
the relaxation flowing up from the floor
through your feet and throughout your body
up to your head.

Tighten your body for a moment
and hold everything
as you inhale
your basic relaxation breath.
Then exhale, and let everything go.

Next,
sit again
with your feet flat,
your spine straight,
and your hands loosely on your knees.

Breathe your basic relaxation breath.
As you exhale,
push all the air out of you,
push your spine straight
against the back of your chair,
pull your stomach and abdomen in
as close to your spine as they will go,
contract your buttocks and thighs.
And hold for as long as you can.

When you have to inhale again,
release everything.
And allow the new air
to fill your body with new energy
and new relaxation
from the ground up.

You may repeat this exploration
three times if you like.
By the third time,
you will have become a new you.
Ready for new work, new challenges,
and new opportunities.

Work ethics

Working
is a lot like
relaxing.

You can't do well at it
by pushing and pressuring yourself.
In fact,
the more you try to do a good job
of working or relaxing,
the less you will succeed.

Never
try to do anything.
Instead,
just let yourself do everything
you want to do.

When you start
releasing your tension
and becoming an open channel
for your energy to flow through,
you are doing the best work you can do
for your employer as well as for yourself.
And rewards and benefits will follow.
Absolutely automatically.
Think about that.

Nutrition relaxation

Nutrition relaxation

Since what we eat
becomes what we are,
it stands to reason:
if you eat
foods that are irritating,
foods that over-stimulate you
and elevate your blood pressure,
foods that overwork your kidneys
and interfere with uric acid elimination,
foods that have high salt, high sugar,
high caffeine, white flour, white rice,
preservatives, and chemical contents,
you will become more irritable
and less relaxed.

On the other hand:
if you eat
foods that are calming,
foods with a natural balance of nutrients,
vitamins, and minerals,
foods like fresh raw vegetables and fruits,
baked potatoes, steamed seafoods, cottage cheese,
yogurt, grains and whole-grained breads,
you will become less irritable
and more relaxed.

To begin with:
Become more aware of what you eat.
Really look at the form and texture
of your food.
Notice what its appearance tells you.
Keep track through the day
of when your highs and lows appear.
Become aware of your snack habits.
Ask yourself when you are eating
if you are really hungry,
or eating because it is mealtime,
or because you have an unidentifiable craving.
Ask yourself what the unidentifiable craving
actually is.

As you sense your food patterns,
consider changing the ones that may be harmful.
Shifting to snacks like nuts, vegetables and fruit juices
instead of candy, doughnuts and coffee
are a few good examples of where to start.

Then experiment with the following explorations.
If you are of reasonably good health,
you can slowly and gradually
find your own nutritional balance.
And relax your body chemistry.
Naturally.

Vitamins

Some vitamins are especially powerful
as natural relaxing agents.

The vitamin B complex group
is the cornerstone
of health, energy, and stress reduction.
It enhances mental clarity,
reduces fatigue and insomnia,
minimizes nervous irritability,
relieves many forms of anxiety,
and should be part of your daily supplement.

Vitamin C
is a major contributor to good health,
and has a fundamental role in relaxation.
After a shock of any kind,
like a death, a fight, an accident,
the entire reserve of vitamin C
stored in your adrenal glands
is exhausted within minutes.
It must be replaced
to restore the normal balance in your body
and to allow yourself to become
fully relaxed.

Vitamin E
restores and rejuvenates your body,
and helps relax nervousness and tension.

Balance the vitamins you take.
Be sure you are getting enough vitamins A and D.
And if you have any questions or concerns,
get the answers you need to relax them.

Become aware on a day-to-day level
of physical changes in yourself
that may be traced to chemical origins.
As you tune into your body,
it will tell you what you need.

Minerals

At least sixteen different minerals
in your body play essential roles
in stress reduction.
Your muscles, brain, glands, hair,
heart, and blood excrete minerals continuously.
So replacing minerals is a high-priority need,
and both seaweeds and kelp are excellent sources.
Both contain more regular and trace minerals
than any other vegetable source.

And some types provide more vitamins than
fish liver oil,
as well as a vitamin-mineral balance
almost identical to that of human blood.

Snacks and extras

All snacks with a high sugar content
raise your energy level for a moment
and drop you back down again,
lower than you were before.
They leave you feeling letdown, dissatisfied,
and tense.

Drinking coffee with candy or cake
compounds the quick-up/quicker-down effect.
Leaving you even more letdown,
more dissatisfied,
and more tense.

Instead,
consider any or all of
these natural and nutritionally relaxing
substitutes for
mid-morning, afternoon, evening, tv or movie
snacks and treats:

Herbal teas.
Nutritional yeast, stirred into any liquid.
Yogurt.
Bran cereals and whole-grain baked goods.
Blackstrap molasses, in tea, milk, or hot water.
Wheat germ, as a cereal, added to your cooking, or in salads.
Seeds, mixed with raisins and nuts,
especially sunflower seeds.
Sprouts from alfalfa, wheat, mung, and soy beans,
in salads, sandwiches, soups, and omelettes.
Lecithin, in tablet or liquid form,
or made into marmalade by blending
one part whole lemon (seeds, skin, and all),
one part honey,
and three parts of liquid lecithin.

Each of these foods
is a snack that tastes good,
a natural tranquilizer,
and a fundamental source of relaxation.

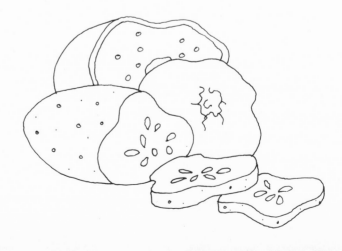

Missing ingredients

Any recipe for a relaxed meal
requires a relaxed cook.

Whenever you rush around your kitchen
radiating tension,
you can be sure that whatever you're making
will reflect back
whatever energy it's taking in
from you.

So whether you're preparing one egg
or a complete dinner
for a party of twenty-four,
the two ingredients most recipes forget are:
Time.
And relaxation.

Allow enough time
to flow with the food-making process.
And to experience each ingredient
and each cooking utensil as an extension
of yourself.
You can always find ways to create enough time.
Simply by starting earlier.

Or by wanting enough time
to stretch each second
into a kind of infinite meditative moment,
and returning to standard time
when you're done.

Allow relaxation
to flavor your food with loving contentment
and peace.
Breathe your basic relaxation breath
as you dice a vegetable,
shake a condiment,
or saute a main course.
Allow the essence of the food
to flow into you as you inhale deeply.
And allow your calmness
to flow back into the food around you
as you exhale.

The difference you'll discover
is more than a matter of taste.

And after you've tried this
in your own kitchen,
you'll become more aware of
what's been missing
or not missing
in your meals away from home.

You'll begin to understand why
some restaurant chefs can do no wrong.
And why the problem with fast-food places
is not what goes into the food
but what gets left out of it.

Something to chew on

Everyone who has been bolting down food
is missing out on a couple of things
you don't have to miss out on anymore.

The first is nutritional.
Part of your digestive process,
the most delicate part,
takes place in your mouth and throat.
Here, many food enzymes that break down
too rapidly
in stomach acid
are absorbed directly
through sensitive epithelial linings.

The more you chew your food
the more you get out of it.
Quite literally.

The second is sensual.
Chewing fully and completely,
using your tongue, your teeth,
and all of your mouth
is a delicious experience.

In terms of pure creature pleasure,
chewing comes in very high
on the all-time list.

See what happens when you
simply roll each bite up along the roof of your mouth
or let it ooze succulently under your tongue
and between your jaws.
It has to be experienced to be believed.

If you've been eating more lately
but enjoying it less,
inhale your basic relaxation breath
before each mouthful.
And chew your way
through the longest, slowest, most mouth-watering exhalation
you can imagine.

You'll find yourself filled
with complete relaxation.

Feeding the Relaxation Reflex

For food to really contribute
to your well-being,
your system must be relaxed enough
to digest, metabolize, and process it
completely.
Before any meal or snack,
feed yourself the Relaxation Reflex.
You'll strengthen it
and it will strengthen you
each time you tell yourself and your digestion:
"Relax... Relax... Relax..."

Driving relaxation

Driving relaxation

Two, three, four, or more times a day,
you probably find yourself surrounded
by the madness of
rushing irritation, blaring horns, screeching brakes,
and potential danger.
Mysteriously,
the most fiercely competitive creatures
you've ever seen
fade into ordinary everyday people
the minute they step out of
their automobiles.

Driving away on-the-road tension
seems almost impossible.

And yet
you can relax yourself,
even when everyone else is
moving much too fast
and feeling much too negative.
Simply by creating and maintaining
a protective layer of relaxation
around you.

The explorations in this section
can keep you as safe as seatbelts
and as comfortable as a cushioned limousine,
by enabling you to relax.

The seat of your tension

Relaxing on the road begins
when you put yourself in the driver's seat
in a totally stress-free way.

Whether your car has
infinitely-adjustable electronic seating
or just one adjustment lever,
here's what to do.

Sit back. And check to see that:
Your back and shoulders
are pressing firmly into the back of your seat.
Your knees are slightly bent
as your heels rest on the floorboard
with your feet positioned over the pedals.
Your hands are resting loosely
on the spokes of the steering wheel
with your elbows dangling down
and lightly brushing against the back of your seat.

Shoulder-to-the-wheel
does not apply to driving your car.
In fact,
most body tension and fatigue
comes from clutching the top of
your steering wheel
with your shoulders hunched forward
and your elbows rigid and stiff.

Most of the time
your hands and wrists can take you
through all your turns
while the rest of you sits back
and enjoys the ride,
completely relaxed.

A head on the road

As you settle into your car
and start it up,
take thirty to sixty seconds to relate to your machine
before you pull out into the street world.

In your car,
you become a completely different entity
than you are on your feet.

You don't need to use
your hands or legs or body
the same way.
Your car becomes the body, the legs,
the motive power source,
while you become the eyes and brain,
the sensory and control system
for a new entity that is both man and machine.

Flow
for a few moments
into this unique bionic relationship.
Merge gently
into your car
and sense yourselves becoming
a single organism.
And notice what happens.

You will drive better
and your car will run better
than ever before.
And you and your car will take care of each other
and keep each other from harm
in ways that will seem unworldly and uncanny.
Until you experience them.

Driving tension away

Various combinations
of heavy traffic, long trips, and past patterns
may cause you to experience
excessive on-the-road body tension.
Now you can relax it completely
as you drive along.
And leave it far behind you.

Begin
by sending a little ray of awareness
to beam and scan over all of you
from head to foot.

Notice where you feel most tense,
most cramped or most uncomfortable.
And start there.

Then move to the next most tense place
and continue all around your body,
using the following techniques,
until you begin to sense
that you are once again
completely relaxed.

Relaxing your legs and feet

Lift your right foot off the gas pedal
and into the space above it.
Straighten your knee as much as you can.
Coast along
as you inhale your basic relaxation breath
and stretch your toes backwards
toward your head.
Hold for just a moment.
Then exhale,
relax your foot,
and shake all the tension out of your toes.

Replace your right foot on the gas pedal
and repeat your basic relaxation breath
as you stretch, relax, and shake
your left foot.

Relaxing your lower back

Keep your legs and feet where they are
and your eyes on the road ahead of you
at all times.

Hold the steering wheel with your right hand
and place your left arm across your lap
with your left hand under your right thigh,
as close to your right hip as possible.

Inhale your basic relaxation breath
and rotate your back
by tightening your left arm
and turning your chest and left shoulder
toward the passenger seat.

As you exhale,
release your hand
and allow your back and shoulders
to sink back into your seat.

Switch hands on the steering wheel.
With your right arm across your lap
and your right hand under your left thigh
as close to your left hip as possible,
breathe your basic relaxation breath
and reverse the stretch
by rotating your chest and right shoulder
toward your door.

As you exhale,
release your hand
and sink back against your seat
in your normal driving position.

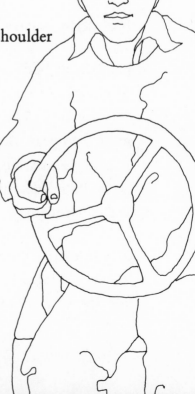

Then
arch your chest towards the steering wheel
with your shoulders pressed back
against your seat.
Inhale.
As you exhale,
press your lower back into your seat
and draw your stomach and diaphragm in
until they feel like
they're pressed against your seat back too.

Repeat this a few times.
And you'll begin to notice that
relaxation has come back
to your back.

Relaxing your shoulders

Inhale your basic relaxation breath.
With both hands on the steering wheel,
hunch your shoulders up
and try to press them
against your earlobes.
Hold the inhalation
and pull your neck in like a turtle.

As you exhale slowly,
let your shoulders melt
into the back of your seat.

Relaxing your neck

With your eyes fixed on the road
in front of you,
let your head fall forward
until your chin is on your chest.

Lift your head all the way back
until your chin is pointing
at the dashboard.
Repeat this a few times.

With your eyes still on the road,
let your head fall sideways
toward your right shoulder.

Lift it slowly against the force of gravity
and let it fall sideways
toward your left shoulder.

Repeat this a few times
until you feel the tension dissolve.

When you come to a stoplight or a toll booth,
finish off the cycle
with a slow deep neck roll
all around
in both directions.

A facial

You can relax your face instantly
and shed all the tension lines
around your eyes,
across your forehead,
and throughout your jaw,
like this.

Keeping your eyes wide open,
scrunch up the rest of your face
until you're looking like
a wrinkled old troll.

Then force your mouth wide open
and stick out your tongue
as far as it will go.
Maintaining the wrinkles and the tension,
stick it out even further
and flag it up to your nose
and down to your chin
like a taxi-meter handle.

Don't even think
about how you look to other drivers.
If they notice you at all
they'll keep a respectful distance away.

Your isolation chamber

No matter what conditions may be like
at home or at work,
your car is one place
where you can always go to be
alone.

Here
in isolation,
you can think whatever you'd like to think,
you can try whatever you'd like to try,
you can be whatever you'd like to be,
as you drive along.

You can scream.
Just roll up the windows
and scream out:
Anger in bestial growls.
Loneliness in mournful wails.
Happiness in excited whoops and laughs.

Whatever you feel,
this is always the place
where you can give it a voice.
A loud, shrieking, raucous, vibrantly alive
voice of its own.

You can sing.
Practice by turning
your basic relaxation breath
into a sound.

Inhale gently,
allowing the air to flow
deep into your diaphragm.
Exhale,
creating musical notes and sounds.

Practice scales.
See how high you can go.
Or how low.

Try an aria, a disco number,
or an old favorite
with the sound vibrating out from your gut
instead of your mouth or throat.
Experience the song of the open road.

You can chant.
Choose whatever sound mantra you like
and chant it
over and over and over and over again
from here to there.
Coordinate your breathing with it.
And let it work its magic.

You can learn.
You can drive yourself to memorize
anything
and lock it permanently in your brain
by repeating pieces of it again and again
like mini-mantras,
and then joining them all together.
Play all your memories back to yourself
like tapes in a cassette deck
as you build your own internalized library
on wheels.

If you learn to use
the full potential of your car
as an isolation chamber,
you'll never mind traffic or traveling.
And you will always emerge
on the other end of your journey
a more complete
and a more completely relaxed human
being.

Breathing through traffic

When traffic stops,
it's time for serious breathing to start.
Practice the alternate breathing cycle on page 32,
but extend your count
with each new breath.

Start with a cycle of
inhaling for two with your left nostril,
holding for eight,
and exhaling for four with your right nostril.
Reverse your nostrils and repeat the cycle.
Then
inhale, hold, and exhale your way up to:
4: 16: 8,
6: 24: 12,
10: 40: 20,
15: 60: 30,
and more.

Inhale.   Hold.   Exhale.

Inhale.   Hold.   Exhale.

Getting caught in traffic jams a lot
can get you to extend your capacity for breathing
and for balancing yourself
so much
that you may actually look forward
to opportunites for turning rush hours
into relaxation hours.

Relaxing fatigue

Becoming fatigued
on a long trip or a long night drive
is unfortunately a common method
for dealing with excessive body tension.
The problem is
that if you fall asleep when your car is moving,
you will not wake up
feeling refreshed.

Relaxing body tension as you drive
will stall off fatigue
and extend your mileage.
But you need to listen
to your body
when it tells you it's had enough
for one day.

Then and there,
if you can stop,
stop.

Pull over
wherever it looks safe
and rest your engine and your self.
Get out for a minute and stretch.
Then sit back down again,
lock the doors,
and just breathe deeply and evenly
or watch the headlights flare by
until you doze off.
Tell yourself to sleep lightly
like a cat,
and you'll wake up
like a cat wakes up.
Completely alert and completely relaxed.

If, for any reason,
you can't stop,
start
changing your driving environment fast.

Move your seat forward or backward
to create more tension and less comfort.
Break your rhythm by driving five miles per hour slower.
Play something you don't like on your radio
and play it loud.

Sing every song you can remember
from 1959
at the top of your voice,
and then move on to another year.
Open a couple of windows wide
and turn off the heater.
Chant to yourself:
"Awake and alive,
that's how I drive."

And as soon as you can stop,
stop.

One for the road

Use the Relaxation Reflex
to keep yourself
alert as well as relaxed,
free and clear of tension and fatigue.

As you drive,
position one or both hands
on the steering wheel
just above one of the spokes
so that the rim is held loosely
in the circle formed
by your thumb and first two fingertips.

Create a blanket of protective energy
around yourself and your car
and recharge it from time to time
by imagining a golden light
streaming down
like water from a carwash
as you inhale.
And by saying,
as you exhale:
"Relax and be safe... Relax and be safe...
Relax and be safe..."
You will be
because you and your car will be
traveling in a state of
complete relaxation.

Family relaxation

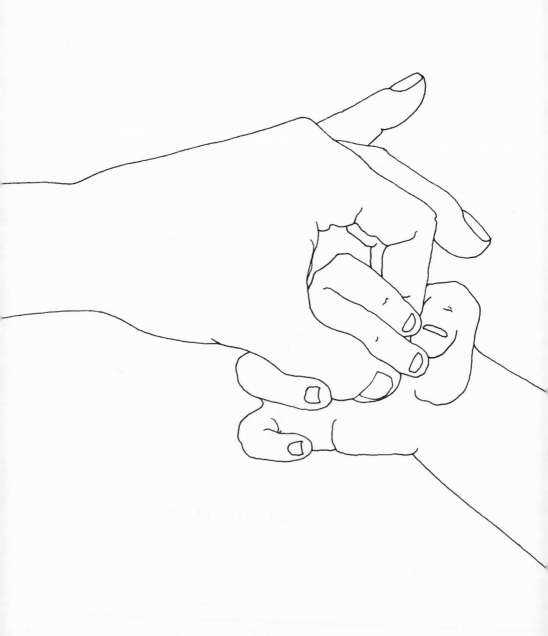

Family relaxation

Be it ever so stressful
or be it ever so relaxed,
there's no space like home.

Your space at home
is always what you make it.
And because you start your day there,
and end your day there,
and spend your leisure time there,
you can now begin to make it
a more relaxing place
to be.
Just so you can feel at home
when you are at home.

Battlegrounds or learning centers
are created and played out
over lifetime patterns based upon
how you and your family choose to be
together.

In this section,
you can explore some of the ways
you and your family can choose to be
completely relaxed
together.

Family feelings

Feelings are facts.
And trusting your feelings
is essential
before you can trust yourself
to be
relaxed.
Whatever you feel
when you're with your family
is all right,
even if you feel you don't like your family.
And whatever you feel
when you're with your family
needs to be
communicated verbally.

Feelings that are blocked inside of you
will seep out
like fumes from food
stored in plastic bags too long.
And fill your environment
with their moods.

Feelings that are released flow on,
leaving open spaces
for love and communication
to flow into.

Any way you talk about your feelings
is better than not talking about them at all.
But some ways produce more positive results
than others.
And the simplest, most direct ways produce
the best results of all.

For instance,
instead of expressing your feelings
with long and tiring monologs
or punishments and threats,
you might just say:
"I feel furious.
Here you are coming home late again
and dinner is ruined."
Or:
"I am sad and disheartened
when I see you have lost another sweater at school."

The fundamental formula
for communicating your feelings
is this:
Tell your family what you see happening around you.
And tell them how you feel about it.

Talking about your feelings freely and fairly
will make it possible
for everyone in your family to know
where they stand with you.

And when everyone in your family knows
where they stand with you,
and where they stand with each other,
it will enable everyone to begin
to become
more completely relaxed.

Family rights

In shared family spaces,
each member of the group has rights.
But the leaders of the family
who pay the rent or mortgage
and who have the ultimate responsibility
for the shared family space itself,
have more rights
about the use of that space
or the property in it
than their children,
or other family members who may be there.

Clearing the air about that issue
clears away tension
fast.

But whenever perception is involved,
rights within a family are truly equal.
And anyone you live with
has the right to see, feel, and react
to things, people, and events,
differently than you.

Watch what happens
when you accept
your child's point of view:
when he's angry at his sister,
or afraid of your favorite aunt,
or crying about a broken toy,
or not willing to share a new gift,
instead of trying to convince him
that his reactions are nasty,
silly, mean, hostile, rude,
or otherwise inappropriate.

Tension thrives
when you deny your children's perceptions
or you allow them to deny your own.
Other than that,
getting into arguments of any kind
over the issue of rights
is a sure way
to give up your own inalienable right
to relax.

Words, words, words

Sense how quickly the level
of your family's tension falls:
When you avoid sarcasm, promises, and warnings.
When you turn threats into choices.
When you erase should and must
from your vocabulary.

When you banish guilt and blame.
When you emphasize what needs to be done now
instead of what was done before.
When you eliminate all labels
and judgmental words,
especially words like good, bad, clumsy, stupid,
dirty, irresponsible, babyish, and klutzy.
When you focus on what you want done
instead of what got done.
When you talk less and listen more.

Words that evaluate,
even when they're praising
and acclaiming
always produce tension.
Recall your own feelings
when they said
you were a little genius
or a living doll
or too good to be true.

Words that describe
what you see
and how you feel about what happened
always flow easily to their mark.
Wouldn't you rather hear
how the expressiveness of your letter
moved her to tears
than
how it was the best letter you ever wrote.

When you talk to your family
as if they are capable people
who do things that sometimes please you
and sometimes create tension in you,
everyone will know what to expect.
And what you can expect back is
a more completely relaxed
family.

Roles and expectations

Don't play them out.
And remember:
When you treat a person, large or small,
as you would like him to become,
he will.

Space

Closeness
within a family group
is wonderful to experience.
But at times,
space
is even more wonderful.
And the more space
you allow
for yourself and for each member of your family,
the more closeness you will feel.
All together.

Physical space comes first.

Everyone, in every home,
needs a space set aside
for retreating.
A place to call his own.
A personal area
where anything goes.
Within reason and without restriction.
A private area
for each family member to have
as a personal sanctuary.

Whether it's a space for
meditating
or studying
or nursing a hurt
or wasting time
or enjoying a special moment of life
or just doing nothing at all
doesn't matter.
Having a space to do it in
is what counts.

If it is at all possible,
each member of your family
will grow and prosper
in a separate room
with a door
that closes.

If you are a large family
in a small house or apartment,
agreeing to share a space
works almost as well.

Set aside one room,
no matter how small it is,
for private space.

You may post a schedule
of reserved time for each person
on the door.
Or negotiate for space inside
on an as-needed basis.
But each of you must feel secure
that some equal time alone
will be available
when you need it most.

As you will find out,
privacy
and time apart
is a holy thing.
No family can relax together without it.

Emotional space
is like physical space
only you don't need to set aside
a room for it.
Instead,
you create your own room for it
all around you.
It's relatively easy
once you know how.
In fact, any child can learn
to do it
and to love it.

You create emotional space
by knowing how you feel,
by letting how you feel
surround you like an aura,
and by taking how you feel seriously.

That means
if you feel angry
and someone else in your family feels happy,
it's all right that way.

You don't have to stop feeling angry
for him.
And you don't have to upset his happiness
or try to change his feelings either.

That also means
if you feel happy
and someone else in your family feels sad,
that's all right too.
You don't have to begin to feel bad
about feeling good.
You can simply acknowledge
that you perceive your loved one's feeling
and express a little sympathy
if you really feel a little sympathy.
And just keep on feeling happy yourself
in your own private emotional space.
Without flaunting it.

Giving yourself permission
to feel what you feel
will relax you.
Giving everyone else permission
to feel what they feel
will relax everyone else.

Look at it this way.
Everyone within your family group
is also a person
within his own space.
Love, honor, and respect that space.
And relax.

Your own family circle

As you try the explorations you have just read
you will notice remarkable changes
in the patterns of your family relationships.
These new bonds
can be lastingly cemented
by the Relaxation Reflex.

Sit on a comfortable rug
with your family,
all cross-legged,
forming a circle so close
that everyone's knees are touching.

Extend your hands towards your knees
with your right palm facing down
and your left palm facing up,
and ask everyone to do the same.

Form circles
with your thumb
and first two fingers of each hand
that interlock with the circles formed
by the people you love
who are seated beside you,
and show everyone else how to do it too.

When everyone in your family circle
is linked together,
close your eyes gently.

Breathe slowly and deeply.
And let the love flow and be received
all around.

As everyone inhales,
sense the love you are sharing
and let it fill your bodies
and fill your lives.

As everyone exhales,
softly say together:
"Relax, I love you... Relax, I love you...
Relax, I love you..."

Remain seated
with your hands joined
in the Relaxation Reflex
for a moment.
You will feel your family roots
intertwined and more deeply connected
than you have ever experienced them
before.

Spirit relaxation

Spirit relaxation

The ultimate step
in the process of relaxing
is simply to be and to believe.
For what you believe you can be,
you can eventually become.

What you believe now isn't so important.
It may change from month to month
and year to year.
That you believe now is essential.
Whether you believe in
the power of nature,
the power of a god
inside of you or outside of you,
the power of the ocean,
the power of the universe,
or the power of your self,
all paths lead you to the same place.

So, whether you meditate
to the rhythm of a novena
and the feel of rosary beads,
or to the sound of waves on the rocks
and the feel of the wind on your face,
the result is the same.

You experience a sense of oneness and integration,
internally and externally,
as you become
spiritually in tune with your beliefs.

Your deity

Find a picture of your favorite deity.
It may be
a painting of Jesus or Buddha or a saint.
Or a photograph of a loved one,
or a very spiritual person who inspires you.
It may be a symbol
if your deity is formless,
or an abstract work of art,
or an impressionistic photograph
with swirls of smoke or colors or clouds.

Whatever the picture is,
sit in a comfortable chair
and place the picture in front of you.
And concentrate on it.
Completely.

Activate the Relaxation Reflex.
And breathe your basic relaxation breath,
letting no outer sounds or inner thoughts
disturb you.

Just look
fully at the picture.
And think
of the divine attributes it represents.
Like love, magnanimity, warmth, kindness,
and extraordinary power.
Then close your eyes
and visualize the picture
printed on the backs of your eyelids.

Breathe your basic relaxation breath
and let calmness and tranquility
flow through every part
of your being.

Air

Sit.
Outside, if it is a beautiful warm day.
Inside by a window, if it is not.
Breathe your basic relaxation breath
and begin to concentrate
on the air all around you.

Become aware
of its formless, nameless, substanceless
vastness.

Allow it to enter you
and fill your body and mind and spirit
with peace.

Beautiful thoughts

To an astonishing degree,
you are what you think.
And thinking beautiful thoughts
can make you a beautiful person.

Try
thinking any one single thought
that you consider beautiful.
It can be a concept,
a place,
or an event.

Sit quietly
and as you breathe your basic relaxation breath
for at least three minutes,
let that one beautiful thought
develop and unfold
from budding to fullness
like the petals
of a flower.

A few everyday beautiful thoughts might be:

Feeling yourself filled with light.
A mountain.
Pine trees.
An island with a crystal lake.
Children singing.
The wind in the willows.
The surf breaking on white coral sand.
Rain on a roof.
The month of May.
The month of October.
Something written by Henry David Thoreau
or Robert Frost or Richard Rodgers.

Try any of these.
Or any of your own.
As you fill yourself with beauty,
you fill your spirit with relaxation.

Your self

You.
You have a body.
And you are your body.
And yet, you are more than your body.

You have emotions.
And you are your emotions.
And yet, you are more than your emotions.

You have thoughts.
And you are your thoughts.
And yet, you are more than your thoughts.

You have spirit.
And in every way,
you are your spirit.
No more, no less.
Your spirit is the energy you have inside
that powers your life.
Your spirit is the energy you send out
as it interacts with people all around you
and their spirits.
It is your self.

Your spirit can range in size
from smaller than a molecule
to bigger than a galaxy,
changing back and forth in size
infinite times
in the time it takes to blink your eye.
When your spirit is small,
you tend to feel like it feels.
Tighter, denser, and more compressed
within your space.

Your friends may point out that
you seem to be in low spirits.
And something elusive
seems wrong.

To soothe your spirit when it's low,
reach in
through the layers of your being
and soothe your self.
Lie down or sit down comfortably.
And set aside at least fifteen undisturbed minutes.

Begin by relaxing your body.
Breathe your basic relaxation breath
and as you inhale,
direct your breath to the part of you
that feels most tense.
Exhale through that part,
floating all the tension away
on the breath.

When your most tense spot
has relaxed,
move on.

Send your breath to your next most tense spot.
And exhale through it.
And move on again.
Until all your body tension
has all blown away.

Next, relax your emotions.
As you inhale, search for the word
that best describes how you feel right now.
As you exhale, affirm it
by repeating it over and over
until the breath is gone.
By now,
just two or three breathing cycles
may be all you need
to identify, affirm, and release
your dominant emotion.

Next, move in to your thought screen
on the inside of your forehead.
Check to see what's playing on it
as you inhale.
And as you exhale,
gently send the thoughts away
and allow your screen to clear.

When all is quiet,
even in the corners of your screen,
ask your spirit to appear.

Your spirit will show up
in many different forms
at many different times.

Each will be real.
And each will really be your spirit.
Ask your spirit what is troubling you.
And your spirit will tell you
what you need to know
and what you need to do.
As your spirit talks with you,
it will grow and lighten and expand.
And your sense of your self
will grow and expand
with it.

When you have finished speaking
together,
you will find your self
and your spirit
soaring.

You may find it interesting
to repeat this exploration
when you already are in high spirits.
Because feeling good
is much more spiritually uplifting
than feeling not so good.

Repeat each step of the process.
Relax your body.
Relax your emotions.
Relax your thoughts.
And ask your spirit to appear on your screen.

This time,
your spirit will tell you
what you are doing right
and help you find ways
to do even more of it.

Through this exploration,
you can always reach out
to your spirit
and enable it to relax and flow
more freely
within and around you.
By letting your spirit move this way,
you are letting your spirit move you.

And through your spirit,
you can reach out and connect with
the god that lives inside of you.
The part of you
that is truly and ultimately
your self.

Beyond your self

There is a world out there.
And a universe beyond the world.
And, while you are the center
and the focal point
of your universe,
there is more to it than that.

Many mystics write
of a universal consciousness
that exists around you.

Many religionists write
of a supreme supernatural force
that is the source of everything.

Many scientists write
of a primal energy flow
that provides the motive power of the galaxy.

Whatever it is,
you can flow into it
and let yourself be
carried along with it
on a vast stream of something that is
more than you are.

You can get in contact with it
by allowing yourself to relax
as a way of life
and learning to let go
of your self.

It's actually easy
to tune into it
and become part of it.
Because you are
part of it.

You don't have to give up your self
or any part of your self.
And you don't become less
or smaller than you are.

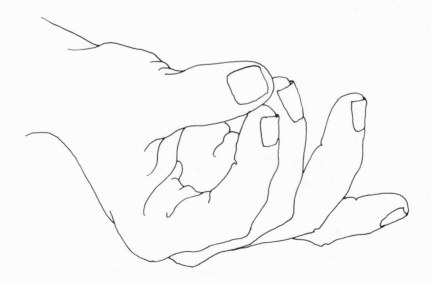

In fact
you find that you are expanding yourself
and becoming more than you were.
As, in the process of expansion,
you relax your ego.
Allowing it to recharge and refresh itself
and to grow ever brighter and stronger.

One way to go beyond yourself
is to simply:
Sit
in a comfortable position
or in a comfortable chair
with your spine straight.

Activate the Relaxation Reflex
and send all outside thoughts gently away.
Then continue to breathe your basic relaxation breath.
Say to yourself on each exhalation:
"I am a part of the universe.
And filled with its energy and vitality, health and wealth.
I am flowing into the universe." And pause.

Say to yourself on each inhalation:
"And the universe is flowing into me." And pause.
Get into the rhythm of your words and your breathing.
And with every breath you take,
repeat the thought.

Each time
you explore beyond your personal limits
in this manner,
you encourage expansion to occur
in a tremendously powerful way.

As you accept the fact
that you are not all alone in the world after all
and as you connect with
and plug into the energy force around you,
you will sense
the dark corners of your mind growing brighter,
your spiritual awareness growing deeper,
and your life becoming more harmonious
and more universally relaxed.

Sensual relaxation

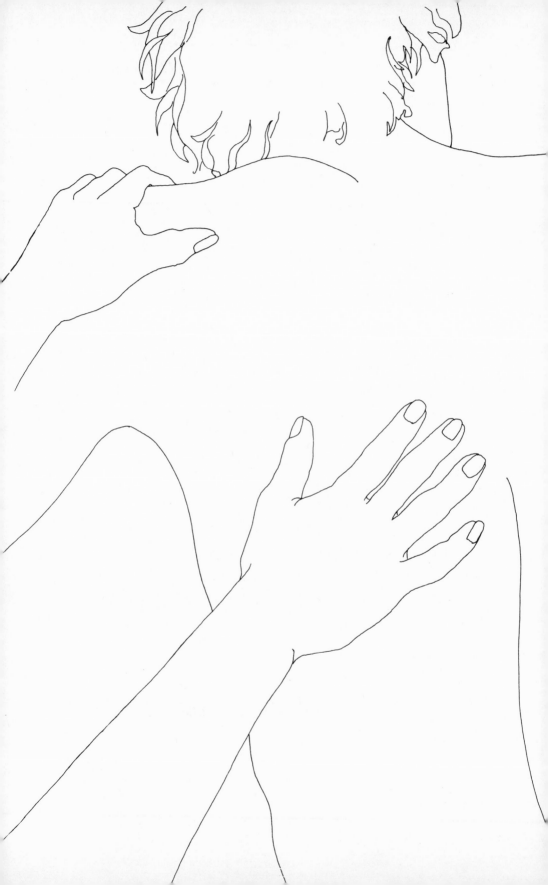

Sensual relaxation

When you are able
to be relaxed and comfortable
and fully at home in your own space,
you can begin to be
relaxed and comfortable
and fully at home with someone else.

This part of the book
extends what you already know
about relaxing yourself
to helping a friend or loved one
relax with you.

Physical relaxation is the focal point.
Because
through touch and caring
and warmth and holding and caressing
in an atmosphere of total emotional openness,
tension between two people
becomes almost impossible to sustain.

As you'll see.

Massage

Massage is the transferring and sharing
of energy
between two people.
The only fundamental rule to follow
is that you like the feeling
of the other person.
Otherwise
you can't transfer and share energy
because you will be tense
and the other person will become tenser.

A massage can be given
in minutes
to a part of someone else
that needs special attention.
Or it can take an hour or two
to cover all the parts
that make up a whole person.
A simple one-zone massage can be given
almost anywhere.
But a longer massage requires
solitude and warmth.
The process will take you and your friend
to a universe where only touch is important.

To oil or not to oil
is strictly up to you and your friend.
Pure natural oils
are more beneficial to the skin
than mineral oils,
and they allow smoother, more flowing strokes.
But you can experiment with both
or neither.

Actually,
you don't have to get all wrapped up
in technique.
It is not important.
If something feels good to the other person,
you will know it
because it will feel good to you, too.
That's the way it always works
best.

Once you begin,
the whole idea is to allow
your energy to merge and flow into
the other person's energy
so that the two of you achieve a oneness.
Be sure you start by activating the Relaxation Reflex.
Sense that you are completely relaxed and breathing
your basic relaxation breath.

The other person will feel your relaxation
and respond to it
by breathing with you.

If he doesn't respond to the rhythm
of your breathing
because his own breathing is tense and shallow,
place your hands softly
on his head or neck
and massage gently until his breathing
relaxes.
It always will if you really want it to.

Use
as much or as little pressure
as you think you need.
Some places need more.
Others need less.
Your own sensitivity
will be your best guide.

If you remember only
that massage is an integrating process
that opens up all the channels to energy flow
and to relaxation,
whatever seems natural and right to you
will be
natural and right.

An instant relaxing massage

Wherever you and your partner may be,
if you sense tension,
take his hand and massage it.

Begin by holding his hand
between both your palms,
forming a connective energy sandwich
as you send thoughts of warmth
and relaxation.

Then
gently pull and stretch and rotate
each finger
from the root to the tip.

Next,
pull down from the wrist,
tracing the lines between the knuckles
all the way to the webs betweeen the fingers.

Knead each webbed pad
as you come to it,
giving special attention
to the web between the thumb and index finger.

Slide
your fingers under your partner's hand
and hold and steady it
as you place your thumbs together
on the top of his hand.
Stretch the back surfaces of his hand
by pulling the top part of his hand down
with the heels of your hands.

Turn
the palm up
and stretch his palm back the same way,
by pulling to the sides
with the heels of your hands.

Then massage his palm
by rubbing the heel of your own palm over it
in a circular motion.

Massage the inside
of your partner's wrist
with your thumbs
and the back of his wrist
with your fingers.

Then,
make a V
with your first two fingers
and use it like a lever
to push back
each of your partner's fingers
from the underside of his hand.

Let yourself improvise.
If anything else seems necessary,
do it.
Then conclude
by replacing his hand between your palms
in another connective energy sandwich.

Notice
how much stronger the connection is now.
And then,
go on to the other hand.

The entire process
may take only a couple of minutes,
less time than it took to read about it.
And you can do it anywhere:
In a car, a meeting, a movie, a party, or a park.
The relaxation effect
is instant and long-lasting.

Head and neck massage

Great pockets of tension lurk
in faces, heads, and necks.
Given just a little quiet and a little time,
here is how you can
open the pockets wide.
And send all the tension away.

Have your partner sit
in a comfortable low-backed chair
which you can stand behind.
Place your hands lightly on his head
to make contact
and to open the energy-sharing circuits.

Move your fingers gently over his head,
lingering, without pressure,
on each neurovascular holding point
for thirty to sixty seconds.
These points,
like acupuncture and shiatsu pressure points,
have far-reaching internal effects
that seem to benefit many other parts
of the body.

Next,
loosen his scalp
with light circular motions of your fingers.

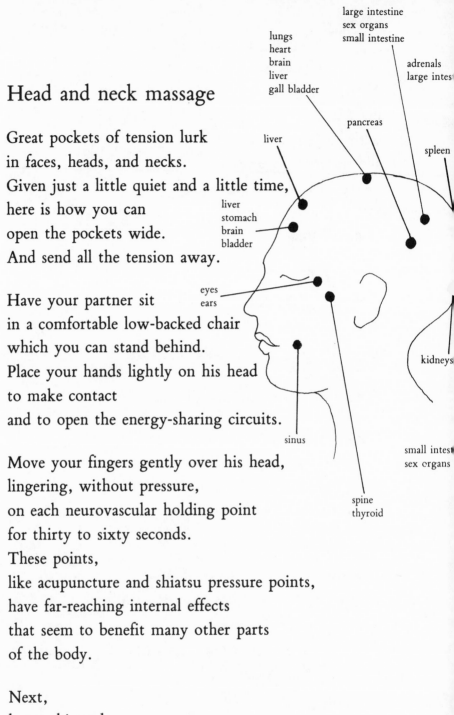

Start at the forehead with your fingertips touching
and work back over the temples to the ears.
Then work your hands back from the ears,
over the top of the head
to the center of the head.

Cover the entire scalp
one section at a time,
working your thumbs and fingers deeply in
toward the cranial bone,
tracing all the sutural paths of the skull,
and loosening all tightness and tension.

Try placing your right hand
on your partner's forehead
and your left hand on the back of his head,
and work your fingers together
until the entire scalp moves loosely
and easily.

Next work your thumbs and fingertips
into your partner's ears and earlobes,
and the furrowed ridges
along the backs of his ears.
Like the hands and feet,
the ears have reflexology points
that can produce beneficial effects
throughout the body.

lungs
heart
brain
liver
gall bladder

small intestine
sex organs
large intestine

spleen

liver

pancreas

eyes
ears

spine
thyroid

sinus

liver
stomach
brain
bladder

Move down
towards the neck.
As you support your partner's chin
with one hand,
press the fingers of your other hand
into the hollow place
between the top of the neck
and the base of the head.
Use moderate pressure and a circular motion.
It is an immediate tension release.

Lightly trace
each of the vertebrae in the neck
down to the shoulders,
and massage circles with your thumbs
just above the shoulder blades,
with your hands resting on top of each shoulder.
Keep your rhythm slow,
your pressure even,
and your breathing slow and deep.

Massage up
the shoulder blade ridge
with your thumbs and fingertips,
closer and closer toward the spine as you
loosen the muscles and connective tissue
by pushing the shoulder blades away
from the center of the body.

If you feel any tension knots,
knead them gently but persistently
with your thumbs or first two fingers
until they dissolve.

Next,
lightly massage the neck
with your fingers.
Be certain that it feels loose
before moving upward to the face.

Relax your partner's face
by working your fingers
from a centerline down through the nose and chin
outward towards the ears.

Start with your fingertips joined
on the chin,
and make small circles
as each hand traces the jawbone
all the way back to the earlobes.

Repeat the motion from chin to earlobes
as many times as you need
until the jaw loosens
and the lips part slightly.

Be sure to work your thumbs
into the connective tissue
near the ears
where the jawbone joins the skull.

Then go back to the chin
and work upwards,
loosening the tight lower lip
and the stiff upper lip
with your fingertips.

Then trace each finger along the cheeks
and back to behind the ears.

Massage the nose
and the hollow space
between the nose and cheekbones.

Then
smooth the skin and tissue under the eyes
all the way back to the ears,
lightly erasing lines, worries, and fatigue
with your fingertips.
Retrace the forehead
from the center
and over the brow to the temples,
pausing long enough to massage each temple.

And then
palm your partner's eyes
for a few moments.

Finish by placing your fingers
over the neurovascular holding point
just above the place
where your partner's eyebrows come together.

Then slide your hands upward
and cup your partner's head between your hands
as you send him waves
of warmth and love and relaxation.

This massage
may last from five to thirty minutes.
It's up to you.
The effects of this massage
may last from a couple of hours
to a couple of days.

A relaxed face, head, and neck
shed years of aging
as easily as they shed tension.
This sharing process
can be tremendously exciting
for both of you.

Foot massage

From the standpoint of relaxation,
massaging your partner's feet
and your own
can be the single most important experience
of all.

Through your feet,
you experience the ground that supports you. ,
Through your feet,
you root yourself to the earth.
Through your feet
and the nerve endings and reflexology points
in your feet,
you can stimulate, relax, and revitalize
the rest of the body.

Massaging the feet is similar
to massaging the hands.
Begin by holding one foot
between your two hands
in an energy sandwich.

Then gently
pull and stretch and rotate each toe
and knead the webbing between each toe.

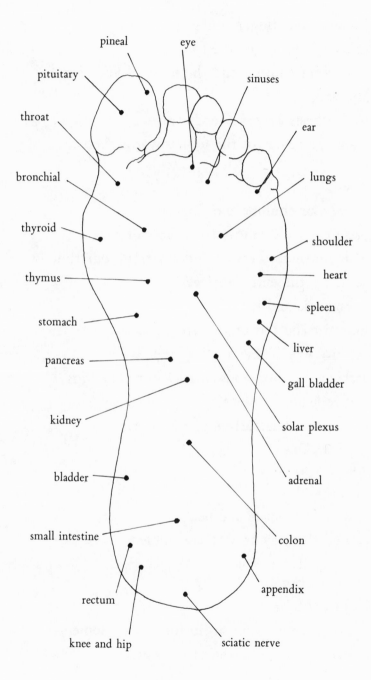

pineal

eye

pituitary

sinuses

throat

ear

bronchial

lungs

thyroid

shoulder

thymus

heart

stomach

spleen

pancreas

liver

gall bladder

kidney

solar plexus

bladder

adrenal

small intestine

colon

rectum

appendix

knee and hip

sciatic nerve

Joining your fingers under the foot,
massage the top of the foot
with your thumbs and the heels of your hands.
Squeeze,
so the heels of your hands travel
from the center of the foot towards the edges.

Then,
with your thumbs and fingers,
press the pads and undersurfaces of each toe.
And continue pressing and rotating your thumbs
all along the entire surface
of the sole and heel.
Be especially thorough here.
Be sure you cover
each of the thousands of tiny nerve endings
and reflexology points
along the undersurface of the foot.

Then work your way
up
around the top of the heel
and all the way around the ankle
and Achilles tendon.

Hold the foot
between your palms again for a few moments
before going on to the other foot.

You must massage both feet evenly
to keep your partner balanced.
So repeat the entire massage step for step,
beginning and ending
with the mingling, merging, energy-sharing sandwich
that integrates the two of you
into oneness.

Body massage

After you've begun
to recognize tension in your own body,
you can begin
to become aware of it in others.

The first step of a full body massage
on a friend or lover
is to tune in and sense
the patterns of tension
in his or her body.

Notice first:
If his shoulders are high, hunched, or held back.
If his face is pinched or tight.
If his motions or gestures are easy and flowing
or sharp, rigid, and exaggerated.
If he is holding himself in or back.

Notice next,
when your partner is lying down
wearing as few clothes as possible
and waiting for you to begin:
If his body sinks into the floor or table
or if he holds some parts of himself up.
If his feet point straight up or fall outward.
If his toes are rigid and bunched up.
If his fingers are tapping or forming fists.
If his breath is shallow and tight in his chest
or deep and relaxed in his diaphragm.

Notice all the zones of tension.
Later you can give them the extra attention
they need.

And then begin
by breathing your basic relaxation breath
as you close your eyes for a moment
with your hands touching your partner's head,
shoulders, feet, or abdomen.

For the rest of the massage,
don't think much about it
or worry about instructions.
Just feel
with your fingers and hands
and let them be your guide.

The whole idea is to connect
all the energy in your partner's body
from hands, feet, head and neck
through the entire body channel
in one smooth effortless flow.

So,
simply take what you've read so far about massage
and apply it,
allowing your fingers and hands
to fill in the details.

There are several books you can buy
to learn different strokes and techniques.
But the best of them
will tell you that whatever feels right
is right.
And warn only
that the spine
should be touched with great care, if at all.

As for strokes, anything goes.

You can:
Stroke with your thumbs, the heels of your hands,
the underside or the knuckles of your closed fists.
Rake with your fingertips.
Make large linear motions with your hands.

You can also:
Make tiny circles with your thumbs
or fingertips
for deeper pressure.
Drum with your fingertips.
Sweep large circles with your forearms.
Chop and hack with the edges of your hands.
Slap lightly with your cupped palms.
Or do whatever else comes to you.

Perhaps sometimes,
you'll start at the head
and work down towards the feet.

Other times,
you may rather work from the feet up.
Just do whatever you sense to be
the way to coordinate and connect
your partner's energy channels and circuits
completely.

And remember:
To deal with the whole body as a whole.
To keep one part of you in contact
with your partner's body
from the beginning of the massage to the end.
To keep communicating nonverbally or verbally.

To let your breathing be deep and natural.
To allow your fingers, hands, and feelings
to guide you.
To have an open mind and watch what happens.
To spontaneously explore and experiment.
And to be.
It's as simple
as that.

Sensual massage

Massage
as you've read about it so far
is a loving experience
but not especially a sexual one.
The energy sharing is an end in itself.

Sensual massage
extends the energy-sharing process
as a prelude to total sexual communication.
It is not
an arousal technique,
oddly enough,
since arousal is the primary side effect.

What it is
is a way
to integrate and diffuse sexual energy
with the energy in the rest of the body
in a smooth, soothing, relaxing buildup
to orgasm.

After you have activated the Relaxtion Reflex,
a whole body massage,
with variations,
is a good place to begin.

As you touch and channel the energy
in your partner's body,
imagine
that your fingers are feathers
or fragile butterflies
and lightly brush them
over your partner's entire body
for as long as you like.

Then
extend your focus
to your partner's erogenous places.
Alternate regular massage strokes
with butterflies and feathers.

Brush, stroke, and flutter over
the toes, the backs of the knees,
the soles of the feet,
the insides of the elbows, the armpits,
the breasts and nipples,
the lips, ears, and back of the neck,
the abdomen, the lower back and buttocks,
the thighs, the insides of the thighs,
the ridge just above the pubic bone,
lightly brushing and connecting with the genitals.

Merge each zone with the rest of the body.
And finally,
merge the rest of the body
with the genitals.
Cover the entire area
with your hands and fingertips,
making tiny circles
that extend from the genitals
over the perenium
to the anus and back again.
Dwell lingeringly on the perenium,
the spot between genitals and anus,
each time.

The combination of
relaxed sensuality and energized sexuality
that you are producing
within your partner's body
will spread throughout your body, too.
As you focus
your hands,
your mind,
and your emotions
on being where you are.
And concentrate only
on giving and receiving pleasure.

Together,
you will find
you are becoming more relaxed
and more responsive
than ever before.

Sexual relaxation

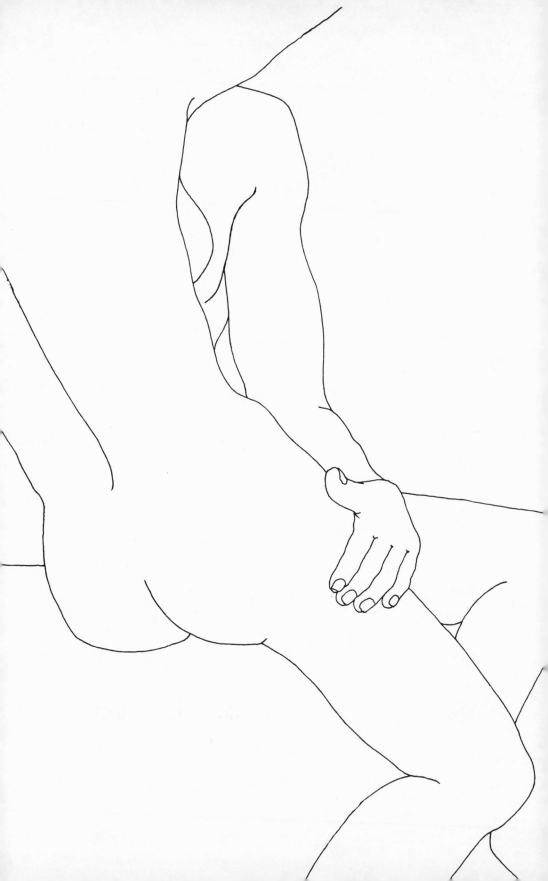

Sexual relaxation

You have already begun
to give your own sexuality
the half chance it needs
to become your greatest source of joy.

By reading this far,
you have been internalizing techniques and concepts
that can produce
and are indeed producing
great and subtle changes within you.

Even if you haven't tried
all of the explorations,
just reading through them
with a free and open mind
empowers them to act.

Think for a moment
how much more relaxed
your lovemaking can become when you:
Let your breathing be rhythmic and deep.
Let yourself go.
Let yourself release wherever you are holding back.
Let yourself be.

Other than that,
the general ingredients
for a free-flowing sexual experience include:
A partner who is right for you.
Attitudes that you can fully accept
without an intellectual/emotional conflict.
And an approach that feels natural, and easy for you.

Only you can determine
what is right, acceptable, natural, and easy.

A partner, for example,
that you are not in complete and open
communication with,
emotionally as well as physically,
cannot contribute to your sexual enjoyment.

Attitudes
that are rigid and anti-pleasure
in their orientation
cannot contribute to your sexual enjoyment.

And an approach to lovemaking
that is forced, tense, artificial, or mechanical
cannot contribute to your sexual enjoyment.

The explorations that follow
will guide you to a place
where lovemaking can be what it really is:
Simple. And natural.
And thoroughly releasing.

Your partner

What counts
is how close and caring and open you are.
And how committed you are,
not in terms of a lifetime
but rather
in terms of being where you are.
And wanting to be where you are
for every moment that you are both there.

Always
like the person you are with.
And love the person you're with, if possible,
in a warm and friendly way
at the very least.

Don't
feel that it is necessary to make love.
You don't have to unless you want to.

Do
feel that you can make love
whenever you really do want to.

You have the freedom to say yes or no,
whichever you feel like.
Whenever your partner means more to you
than a quick escape,
you will always know the right answer
at the right time.

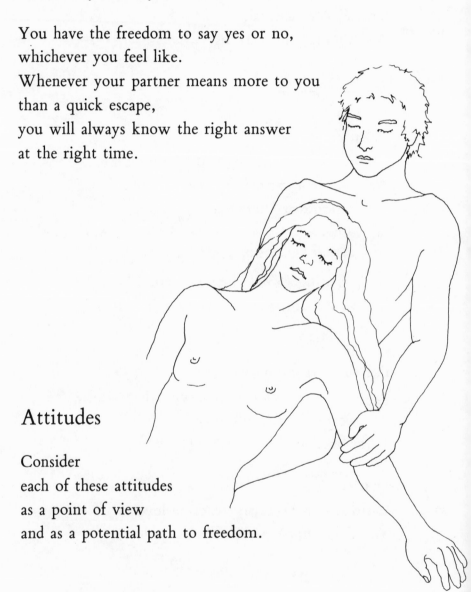

Attitudes

Consider
each of these attitudes
as a point of view
and as a potential path to freedom.

Become aware
of which ones you agree with.
And which ones you don't.
And ask yourself
why you agree
or why you don't.
Right now, by the way,
is the only time
you will want to use your mind
in a sexual exploration.

Attitude 1. Making love
is a good thing.
One of the functions of your body
is to tell you whether something is good for you
or not.
When your body feels alive and singing,
and free and responsive,
you know you are doing something right.

Attitude 2. Responsibility
for sexual excitement and enjoyment
begins and ends
with you.
You can't make anyone else do anything,
even enjoy lovemaking.
And you can't make anyone else feel anything,
even good.

Anytime you begin to think
that it is your duty
or your mission in life
to help or to teach your partner to respond,
you are invading his space
and asking for a disaster.

Attitude 3. Opening your awareness
to include your partner
is entirely different
than putting pressure on him to enjoy
lovemaking.
As you experience feelings in your own body
and allow them to build towards a peak,
become aware
of the effect of your partner's presence on you
and how you are interrelating
with each other.

Attitude 4. Be aware
that you are exposing your feelings
as well as your body.
Leave nothing to chance.
Assume nothing.
Your partner,
even after years and years of being with you,
will not magically know
what you want from him
or what it takes to give you pleasure.

Forget the expectation
that if your partner really loved you
he would know how to satisfy you.
He'll know how if you tell him how.
Openly and without embarassment.
Mindreading is a trick for nightclubs and tv.

Attitude 5. Regardless
of how you make love,
let neither of you be the active partner
all the time
and neither of you be the passive partner
all the time.
Let the role of leadership flow
back and forth,
back and forth,
naturally and spontaneously.
In lovemaking,
you don't have to be on top
to be on top.

Attitude 6. Always listen
to your body.
And give your body what it asks for.
If you know what pleases you,
ask for it.

Teach your partner how to give you
wild and joyous and totally exuberant
pleasure.
If he's slow to learn,
give him a demonstration.

Attitude 7. A highly developed
sense of pleasure
combined with
an equally highly developed
sense of play
will lead you to lovemaking
where complete excitation and oneness
and release
can be
followed by complete relaxation.

Body tension

The places in your body
where you are holding onto energy
instead of letting it flow freely
will haunt you
when you are making love.
The most common tension areas
and explorations to guide you
through them and beyond them
follow.

Most of the tension-releasing techniques
are so simple you can do them anywhere
for practice,
day or night.

Breathing

Your basic relaxation breath will help you
experience sexual fulfillment
by relaxing your body
and freeing it for full responsiveness.

One variation of your basic relaxation breath
for lovemaking
is to add pelvic motion
to your breathing rhythm.

As you inhale and hold,
rock your hips and pelvis back.

As you exhale,
thrust your hips and pelvis forward.
Inhale... rock back.
Exhale... thrust forward.

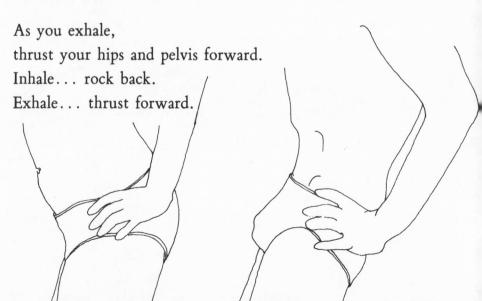

Make the coordination between breathing
and moving
as smooth and natural as you can.
In nature,
before man-made tensions,
this was the flowing rhythm of love.
And it still is.

Pelvic energizing

If you don't have
a full sense of awareness in your pelvic area,
your lovemaking will reflect it.
A pelvis that feels numb to you
will feel deadening and inert
to your partner.

The pelvic breathing variation
of your basic relaxation breath
will help.
So will this.

Lie on a mat with your knees up
and breathe your basic relaxation breath.
Inhale and hold.

And as you exhale slowly,
lift your hips slightly
and lightly tap your pelvis on the floor
about twenty or thirty times.

Then turn over on your stomach,
press the soles of your feet against a wall,
and stabilize yourself
by breathing your basic relaxation breath.

Inhale and hold.
And lift your pelvis
by arching your lower back slightly
and coming up a little on your knees.

As you exhale slowly,
gently bounce your pelvis on the floor
at least twenty or thirty times.

Lie on your back again
with your knees bent and your feet flat
and breathe your basic relaxation breath.
Become aware of any emotions
you may have released
and experience them as they flow freely.
Sense the tingling and reawakening
of your pelvic area.
Enjoy it now.
And enjoy it later with your partner.

Genital breathing

If your genitals
don't feel fully alive and vibrant with energy,
try this with an open mind.
It will open your genital area to contact.

Lie down or sit down
and breathe your basic relaxation breath
with the rocking pelvic motion added.
Imagine
that instead of inhaling and exhaling
through your nose,
you are inhaling and exhaling
through your genitals.

As you inhale and rock your pelvis back,
imagine that the air is
entering through your penis or vagina
and rushing upward
to expand your diaphragm, rib cage, and chest.

As you exhale and thrust your pelvis forward,
imagine that the air is
flowing out of your penis or vagina
as your diaphragm flattens
and your rib cage and chest lower.

Imagine all the tension
flowing out of your penis or vagina
with every exhalation.

Genital breathing
will always focus awareness and energy
in your genitals.
And allow you to fully sense
your own sexuality.

Genital energizing

Try the genital breathing exploration
in a squatting position
with your feet flat on the ground,
your elbows between your knees,
pressing them open,
and your palms together
in front of you, as if praying.

Stay in this position
for at least three minutes
once a day.
You'll charge
your genitals
with energy
and at the same time
leave them feeling
refreshed and relaxed.

Premature ejaculation

If you are a man
with an excitation problem
that causes premature release,
try this simple solution.

Concentrate on
coordinating your pelvic movements
with your basic relaxation breath
from the very beginning of your lovemaking.

And add one variation:
As you inhale, rock your pelvis back
as before.
As you hold, hold your pelvis back
in a cocked and ready position.
And as you exhale, thrust your pelvis forward
as before.
But,
before you inhale again,
make a special effort
to relax your anus.
Releasing your anal muscles
before you thrust back again
will hold your ejaculation back
very effectively
and in a very relaxed way.

If you get carried away
and forget this,
and you are caught very close to climax,
pause
before the orgasm spreads over you,
press one or two fingers hard against your perenium,
and breathe your basic relaxation breath.
As you stroke and caress your partner
with your other hand,
keep your attention focused on your breathing
and allow it to slow down.

Basic relaxation breathing
can solve the majority of
problems involving premature orgasm
by relaxing you completely
before the problems start.

Vaginal contraction

When a woman can mentally connect
with her vagina,
she can learn to tightly grip
her partner's penis
and stimulate it
by contracting and releasing
her vaginal muscles.

This technique can be an incredibly erotic contribution
to lovemaking.

To connect with your vaginal muscles,
you can practice this simple exploration
when you are sitting, standing, lying down,
or anywhere at all.
Just breathe your basic relaxation breath.
As you inhale and hold,
tighten your vagina
as if pulling it up and inward. And hold.
As you exhale,
release your vaginal muscles.

Continue to contract and relax
your vagina
for as long as you wish.
You can't overdo it.
And the more you do it,
the more the effects
will astonish and delight your partner.

Emotional sexual tension

Sex,
for many people,
has a lot of tension and stress and anxiety
connected with it.

Why that happens
is not as important as the fact
that it happens.

To release emotional tension
and let go
and be
does not have to be
difficult.

You can simply decide
to let go of misconceptions,
worries about performance
and expectations,
and give yourself permission
to be
where you are.
Not in yesterday or last year
or when you were twelve years old.
Not in five minutes or an hour from now
when, heaven help you,
you'll try to have an orgasm.
Maybe.

Forget your past, forget your future.
Allow yourself to remember only
to be
where you are
when you are there.

Practice
becoming aware of what you are experiencing
without analyzing it
or judging it.
If you are touching your partner's skin
and you are aware only of
the soft silky feeling under your hands
and the feathery touch of body hair,
you can't be aware of tension or stress
at the same time.
And you can't be affected by it.

Let yourself be
completely carried away
by all the beautiful sensations of the moment.
And you'll forget everything else.

Sex and the Relaxation Reflex

Most fears and anxieties about lovemaking
show up in a particularly tense
part of your body.
An anxious stomach, for example,
can have a devastating effect
on an erection.

To relieve the pressure,
simply inhale your basic relaxation breath,
join your thumb and first two fingers
and recall the effects
of your complete relaxation cycle.
As you exhale,
say to yourself:
"Relax, stomach, relax... Relax, stomach, relax...
Relax, stomach, relax..."
And sense the anxieties dissolve.

Similarly,
a fear of penetration
can cause a vagina to become almost impenetrable
or, at the very least,
produce unnecessary pain
when a penis tries to enter.

To release the tightness,
at the moment of contact,
breathe your basic relaxation breath
and join your thumb and first two fingers together.

As you inhale,
imagine the feeling of
your complete relaxation cycle
flowing warmly through your entire body
from your toes to your head.

As you exhale,
say to yourself:
"Relax, vagina, relax... Relax, vagina, relax...
Relax, vagina, relax..."

And let it be
as you allow the fear, and tension, and pain
to dissipate into nothingness
and the beauty of the experience
to fill you with love and excitement.

Become aware
as you are making love,
whenever a part of you seems to be responding
inappropriately.
If any tension is involved,
activate the Relaxation Reflex
immediately,
and send all the tension in that part of you
away.

Holding back

Sometimes tension develops and spreads
so quickly,
all of you seems to be holding back.
And an overall feeling of tightness
begins to overcome you.

Right at that point,
when you feel the holding-back start,
stop.

Go back to what you were doing
just before the tension started.
Join your thumb and first two fingers
and activate the Relaxation Reflex.

Let yourself experience the moment fully.
Then keep breathing your basic relaxation breath.
Add on your pelvic motions.
Become aware of all the sensations
of the moment.

And go on to the next moment.
And be.

Erections lost and found

The best way
to maintain an erection
is not to try
to maintain an erection.

If you can let your penis be,
it will let you be.
Avoid getting sidetracked by technical details.

If you tried, for instance,
to focus fully
on the process of walking
and how first you put your foot down
and then how you shifted your weight
from your heel to your toe,
you'd become confused.

Then if you tried
to concentrate on
how you pushed off from your toes
and bent your other knee
as you placed your other foot down,
you would never get anywhere at all.
You certainly wouldn't be able to walk
smoothly and easily
through the aisles of a supermarket
or to the corner and back.

Focusing on too many technical details
causes all the sensations to vanish.
And you need those sensations.
Because they
will maintain your erection for you,
without your doing anything at all
but just being there.

If you by chance forget all this
and allow technical details to cause
the loss of your erection,
try thinking of the wildest way
you can imagine
to get it back again.
And ask your partner to do it for you.

Or
try giving your penis permission
not to be erect.
Tell it that it is perfectly all right.
and watch what happens.

Many women enjoy
the process of transforming a soft penis
to an erect penis
with their hands or mouths or breasts
or inner vaginal contractions.

And if your partner is enjoying the process,
join her.

Be there with her,
enjoying all the sensations of the moment,
as you breathe your basic relaxation breath
and become aware of how you feel.

If you are fully where you are,
with the moment and with your partner,
your penis will be there too.
And your penis will take care of itself.
Phenomenally.

Intellectual sexual tension

Here is how to handle it
in two words:
Forget it.

Lovemaking is no place for thinking.
It's for feeling and sensing only.
Feeling creates orgasm.
Intellect creates distance and detachment.
Let your body do all your thinking for you.
Save your intellect for later
when it can do you some good.

For now,
lose your head completely.
And let yourself be.

Touch

Touch your partner
with your fingertips, your hands, your toes,
your nose, your tongue, your lips, your teeth,
your genitals, your nipples.
Touch
with any part of you that feels good.

Touch your partner's body as a whole.
Temples, scalp, cheeks, gums, tongue,
face, neck, elbows, abdomen,
knees, feet, thighs, armpits, breasts.
Connect
all the energy in your partner's body.
Then go on to the genitals, perenium, and anus.

Or try it the other way around.

The point is
to merge and connect
your partner's sexual energy and body energy
with your own
before you merge and connect
your partner's body
with your own.

Lovemaking

By now,
you've taken in all the input you need
and explored
all the explorations you need
to bring you to this point.

The next step
is to put it all together
in your own experience.
Without effort, concentration, or strain.

Each time you make love,
it's different.
So no single approach or set of techniques
can guide you anywhere
but to rigidity and artificiality.

There is always a time and a place
to make love
for five minutes or for five days
or for any time between the two extremes.

The basics to keep around
for reference
are these:

Hold your partner.

Touch and stroke
and caress a lot.

Let go
and be
together.

Lovemaking is sharing and trusting.
It's also fun.
Enter fully into it.
And your body will take care of the rest.
And the relaxation that follows.

Orgasm

In the section on thought relaxation,
you explored various ways
to focus on one thing at a time
to release your mind
from its constant chatter and clutter.

Yogis, mystics, and spiritual people
practice for years
to achieve perfection of this blissful state.
You can achieve it
instantly and automatically
each time
you let yourself go
into orgasm.

Whenever you are climaxing,
you cannot possibly be anywhere else.

Orgasm is
a condition of complete focus on one point.
A timeless moment
that consumes your entire being,
totally filling you and fulfilling you.

You may see colors or stars.
You may hear turbulent crashing waves.
You may feel the earth move.
Or you may just black out.
It's entirely possible,
as you allow orgasmic energy
to fill your body
and expand your senses,
that you will hear colors,
or feel the touch of music,
or experience psychic phenomena.
An unlimited garden
of joyful sensations
will begin to grow all around you.

You are
in the ultimate meditational state
where you can't think of anything else
but the one incredible point in time
that you are experiencing.

Because
you receive all the benefits of meditation
without any of the mental work
or intense concentration,
and because
you experience a complete physical involvement
in which your whole body
is fully connected,
fully activated,
and then fully released,
lovemaking is
the ultimate relaxation.
And orgasm is
the ultimate means of attaining it.

Living relaxation

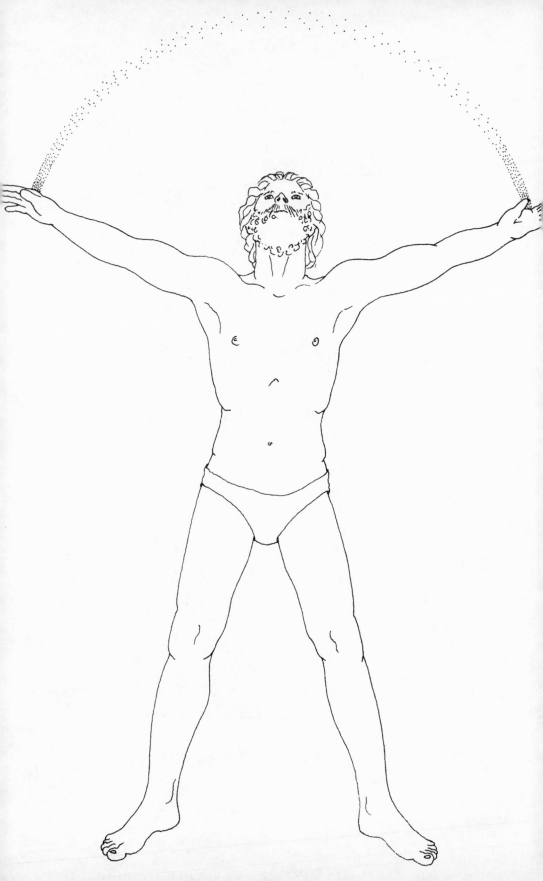

Living relaxation

You will find
as you try the explorations you have read
that your overall approach
to living in the world
can become more relaxed,
less fearful, less guarded.

You will become more and more able
to guide your own life
and to handle
the effects of other people and events
on your life.

It will happen all by itself
as you become more and more accepting
of yourself as you are
and more and more responsible
for your own being.

It will keep happening and expanding
as you continue to use the exploration techniques
to keep your own being
relaxed.

Don't hold back.
Experiment with the explorations.
Try everything you've read
at least once
just to see what happens.
And make a note
of which explorations
work best for you now.
And later.

Remember that you are dealing
with concepts that can provide you
with complete protection
against external and internal forces
that tense, irritate, and annoy you.

As you increase your awareness
of your own body, mind, emotional, and spiritual
patterns,
you will know which areas
need the most work and the most reinforcement.

Realize
that as your life opens
and as you become more and more
completely relaxed,
you will sense more strongly
subtle ever changing cycles within yourself.

You will begin to know
when you feel a little more up
and a little more down,
a little more physically worn,
a little more intellectually fatigued.

You will also begin to know
when your relaxation needs are
purely emotional, sexual, business, mental,
spiritual, or nutritional.
And when they involve
combinations of factors.

Your cyclical ebbs and flows
are as normal as the tides of the ocean.

They explain why
some of the explorations
work some of the time
and why other explorations
work other times.

You can chart yourself and your progress
at periodic intervals.
And become aware of your own cycles.

However,
no matter where you are at,
these four explorations work all of the time.

1. Your basic relaxation breath.

2. The Relaxation Reflex.

3. Asking yourself "How do I feel right now?"

4. Asking yourself "What do I want right now?"

Every other exploration
will help you grow and evolve and flow
in its own time and place.
Contributing
in big broad abstract ways
and tiny specific concrete ways
to enhancing and beautifying and enriching
your life.

Right now,
join your thumb and first two fingers together.
Inhale your basic relaxation breath
and visualize
a wave of complete relaxation
flowing through you from your toes to your head.
Exhale
and say to yourself:
"Relax... Relax... Relax..."

You now have the whole idea.
You now know everything you need to know.
So:
Let yourself be completely relaxed.
Let yourself be completely yourself.
Let yourself be.

Afterword

Afterword

A lot of people who haven't seen me for a few years are going to wonder how Steve Kravette, the uptight adman who was so tense he stuttered at meetings, happened to write a complete book about relaxation.

The answer is he didn't.

The person who Steve Kravette the uptight adman became wrote the book. And the book describes most of the experiences and explorations that happened along the way.

The reason for the book is a story in itself.

During the early part of my journey from there to here, I met and fell in love with a yoga teacher named Dorothy Kerzner. Dorothy specialized in physical relaxation exercises and massage. She just happens to be so good at inducing relaxation that during a class on board the ocean liner Queen Elizabeth II, she dropped a group of students into a near-alpha state right in the middle of all the commotion on the shopping deck. Which takes a whole lot of talent.

I started to go to Dorothy's yoga classes just to be around her but found myself responding to the breathing and relaxation concepts on an almost cellular level and in a fundamental and strangely accelerated way.

Within six months I was teaching with her and introducing and testing lots of original material, including the Relaxation Reflex, which we developed together. Soon after, I began to write this book for Dorothy, hoping that it would become the means by which we would live and work together.

But the relationship ended. When it did, I was no longer Steve Kravette the uptight adman. I was what I am. And I had put together a wonderful book that offers all the techniques you need to know to completely relax yourself in every area of your life so you can be what you are, too.

I developed much of the material in this book myself. But some of it, the body relaxation and massage explorations in particular, is based upon my teaching and learning experiences with Dorothy Kerzner. Many of the emotion relaxation insights are based upon my personal experiences with Dr. Nathaniel Branden, a man I consider to be one of the most gifted group and weekend-intensive therapists around. Still other parts of the material were suggested by my paper friends, the thousands and thousands of books that share my home with me. Especially those by the following authors who came to me just when I needed them most: Richard Bach, Harry Browne, Haim Ginott, Gay Hendricks, Richard Hittleman, Alexander Lowen, Marcia Moore, Jane Roberts, Jack Lee Rosenberg, Anne Kent Rush, and David Smith.

To the small number of people who have asked me how they could be sure the book really works and who have suggested that I get a well-known expert to endorse it and write an introduction, my answer is this:

The world's most important and most knowledgeable expert lives inside each of you. And that is precisely who this book is written for. By trying the explorations I describe, you and your own private expert will discover for yourselves all the calming, soothing benefits this book can bring. Just as my own private expert and I discovered them all along the way to Complete Relaxation.

COMPLETE MEDITATION

Steve Kravette

Complete Meditation presents a broad range of metaphysical concepts and meditation techniques in the same direct, easy-to-assimilate style of the author's best-selling *Complete Relaxation*. Personal experience is the teacher and this unique book is your guide. The free, poetic format leads you through a series of exercises that build on each other, starting with breathing patterns, visualization exercises and a growing confidence that meditation is easy and pleasurable. Graceful illustrations flow along with the text.

Complete Meditation is for readers at all levels of experience. It makes advanced metaphysics and esoteric practices accessible without years of study of the literature, attachment to gurus or initiation into secret societies. Everyone can meditate, everyone is psychic, and with only a little attention everyone can bring oneself and one's circumstances into harmony.

Experienced meditators will appreciate the more advanced techniques, including more sophisticated breathing patterns, astral travel, past-life regression, and much more. All readers will appreciate being shown how ordinarily "boring" experiences are really illuminating gateways into the complete meditation experience. Whether you do all the exercises or not, just reading this book is a pleasure.

Complete meditation can happen anywhere, any time, in thousands of different ways. A candle flame, a daydream, music, sex, a glint of light on your ring. In virtually any circumstances. *Complete Meditation* shows you how.

ISBN 0-914918-28-1
309 pages, 6½" x 9¼", paper

$12.95

EXPAND YOUR PSYCHIC SKILLS

Enid Hoffman

In this sequel to her best-selling *Develop Your Psychic Skills*, Hoffman shows you how to use your inate psychic abilities to improve your daily life and your relationships with other beings. Huna concepts, along with dozens of techniques, exercises, games and meditations are included to help you fully utilize your inner resources. Psychic healing, working with crystals and gemstones, communicating telepathically with people and animals, heightening creative powers, and eliminating old behaviors that are interfering with your personal growth are just a few of the areas covered.

ISBN: 0-914918-72-9
144 pages, 6½" X 9¼", paper $9.95

Steve Kravette is a freelance writer who lives in Cohasset, Massachusetts, where he swims year round. Since the publication of *Complete Relaxation*, he has written two additional books: *Complete Meditation* and *Get a Job in 60 Seconds*. He is currently working on other books in the self-help and self-knowledge fields and is involved in relaxation workshops and career counseling.